Darlene,
What a joy to have you as
a neighbor!
I pray you'll be drawn even
closer to God by reading this!

Behold, God's Word Works
Modern Day Stories of Miracles, Parables, & Wonders

Blessings!
Pamela Jo Nelson
pjnelson2002@yahoo.com

Pamela Jo - 509-398-5038
Leigh - 253-468-5760

Amazon.com

Behold, God's Word Works

Modern Day Stories of Miracles, Parables, & Wonders

Pamela Jo Nelson

Behold, God's Word Works

© 2014 by Pamela Jo Nelson

Unless otherwise noted, all Scripture quotations are from the King James Version of the Bible.

Some Scripture quotations are taken from THE AMPLIFIED BIBLE, Old Testament copyright 1965, 1987 by the Zondervan Corporation. The Amplified New Testament copyright 1958, 1987 by the Lockman Foundation. Used by permission.
Note to reader, this version has many ( ) and [ ] inserted in the text to help capture the full meaning behind the original Greek and Hebrew.

Some Scripture quotations are taken from THE MESSAGE. Copyright 1993, 1994, 1995, 1996, 2000, 2001, 2002. Used by permission of NavPress Publishing Group.

ISBN-13: 978-1500235062

Dedication

This book is dedicated to the One, *Who being the brightness of His glory, and the express image of His person, and upholding all things by the word of His power, when He had by Himself purged our sins, sat down on the right hand of the Majesty on high.*
Hebrews 1:3

Table of Contents

Acknowledgements

My sincere gratitude to Geoff Bullock for writing the beautiful and powerfully moving song, "The Power of Your Love.," Thank you for giving me permission to use your song in this book. [God Sang! pg. 110]

Thank you, Heidi Scott, for helping me edit this book with your wisdom and enthusiasm. And thank you for letting me put the Table of Contents as candlesticks. I hope it will make it easier for readers to make notes about the stories. Watching the "candles" grow encouraged me.

Thank you, Jeanette Munter, for working so hard on the cover and for being such a loving friend for decades.

I must thank my husband, Leigh, for your strong encouragement to write this book, for your computer savvy help, for your tremendous help with the cover, and for your patience. Most of all, thank you, Leigh, for having the courage to let me tell the truth about our lives. We'll pray that many others will learn from our painful past!

To my children, Adam and Rebekah, thank you so much for being the first people to whom I could unabashedly reveal and teach about my love of God. You are remarkable adults, powerful prayer warriors, and generous loving children of the Most High God.

I sincerely thank all my friends and family who have prayed so earnestly for this book to get written. Praise the Lord!

Introduction

What if you had an exceedingly wealthy relative who died and left the entire estate to you, yet a dishonest attorney had appointed himself as executor and he was meagerly doling out a small pittance to you? How would you know what you were legally entitled to, unless you read the will? Chances are very good that this is exactly what is happening to you!

Someone has died, Jesus Christ, and He has left a wonderful will for you, filled with benefits. Yet the vast majority of people, including Christians, are *not* receiving what has been left to them in the will, or last testament. That will was executed by the blood of the Son of the living God and was actually designed to meet every single need of every single person on earth! The reason it isn't happening is *not* the fault of the One who left the will.

The ruthlessly dishonest executor is mankind's arch enemy, the father of lies, who never stops trying to hide, steal, and destroy the truth in the will, because he knows that truth sets us free from evil (John 8:32). Your enemy also knows that God's truth has the power to transform desperate, lonely, broken, empty lives into amazing Believers that go from victory to victory and who are actually changed into glorious images of the dear Son of God (II Cor. 3:18). So, of course he does *not* want the truth in the will to be known.

Here's the fantastic news, and the catch—you must *know* what the will says and you must follow the instructions. Then you will discover that God's Word works! I highly recommend that you take the time to look up the referenced verses throughout this book, each time asking God to show *you* what He wants *you* to see.

I would encourage you to start treating your Bible as if it really is the last will and testament of Jesus Christ (Heb. 9:15-17). It is! The will is valid, the Holy Spirit has been appointed to be your true executor, and you can exercise faith to receive all the great and precious provisions that have been left to you (II Peter 1:4). It's that simple and yet we have made it so difficult.

For over 40 years I have treated God's Word like a will, a love letter, an instruction manual for life, and a treasure map. I've been experiencing the joys and generous provisions of the will. The most wonderful provision of all is that God has revealed so much of Himself and His ways to me. He strongly desires that for you too.

I pray that as I share personal examples of God's wonderful and amazing provisions to me, it will spark your desire and faith to receive what God wants for *you*. I assure you that it's exceedingly abundantly more than you can even imagine (Eph. 3:20).

Remember, God isn't practicing. He's already perfect and everything God does is perfect. That includes His plan for your life. Unfortunately, most people are settling for God's permissive will rather than His perfect will for their lives. There is a *huge* difference! [Perfect or Permissive Will pg. 130]

Maybe this illustration will help you to understand what many people, perhaps even you, are spiritually doing today. Imagine that a poor man saved every cent he could, until he had saved enough for the lowest fare on a cruise ship. He bought his ticket and had just enough money left to buy some jerky and crackers. During the entire cruise, he slipped into his tiny room at meal times to eat a small piece of jerky with a few crackers.

Finally as the ship reached the final port, the steward approached the man and said, "I noticed that you never came into the dining rooms or requested room service. Was there a problem with our food?"

The poor man honestly answered, "Well, you see, I spent all my money on the ticket. I couldn't afford to buy any of the ship's food."

Amazed, the steward replied, "Didn't you know that when you purchased the ticket, the meals were included?"

Far too many people today act the same way in spiritual matters. They do believe that Jesus purchased their ticket to heaven by dying on the cross to forgive their sins. However, they are absolutely oblivious to all the provisions, protection, and blessings that are to accompany each of us on the journey. The One who purchased our ticket for us, also included everything that we could possibly need in every situation that we'll ever face!

When a person really realizes the truth about what kind of a life God intends this journey to heaven to be, they become beacons of light in a dark world. They're allowing God to bring His will to earth, as it is in heaven.

Once you understand that truth, I believe you will sincerely desire to read the Bible. It won't be because you are "supposed to" read it, that attitude just makes you a "page turner." Instead you will want to read God's Word, you will need to read it, and nothing else will satisfy you like hearing from the living Almighty Lord God!

Dear Reader, I hope that you will pant for the Bible and pant for the God of the Bible like the deer pants for water, in Psalms 42:1. That's what will happen when you know that God's Word works!

What a Sacrifice

*W*ear shorts to church? Ugh! As a self-conscious, plump 11-year-old, setting up tents in the pouring rain had been more fun to me than going to church in shorts. The bus rumbled from our Olympic Peninsula Girl Scout camp to picturesque Port Townsend, WA where we could attend our church of choice. We were all wearing our Girl Scout uniforms, including the dreaded shorts.

Fighting back panic that I'd be a spectacle, I walked alone up the steps to the Presbyterian Church. That was the only church I had attended in my family's rare visits to church. The hours were posted on the door. Oh no! Church had already begun. I wouldn't dare enter in late, especially wearing shorts.

I quickly turned and saw a group of shorts-wearing scouts heading towards another church. I dashed off to join them thinking about safety in numbers. We proceeded into a small Methodist church. As I slid into a wooden pew beside the other scouts, I was amazed to see such simplicity inside of a church. Instead of ornate carvings and elegant stained glass windows, this church had plain white walls on three sides.

The only thing I saw on the front wall was a picture of Jesus' face. He didn't looking effeminate or emaciated like in other pictures I'd seen. Instead, Jesus looked like a real rugged guy with exuberant joy shining out of His eyes as He looked up adoringly at His Father. I was transfixed by the power of Jesus' emotions. I don't think that I had ever considered His emotions before that day.

As a young child I had been taken to Sunday school enough to have heard about Jesus dying on the cross, but, until that moment, it had never occurred to me that His death was such a painful emotional sacrifice.

Only a few months earlier, my Grandma Myrtle had died. Her death was a huge loss to me, because in my anger-filled, alcoholic family, Grandma Myrtle was the one person in my life that really loved me and enjoyed me. When she died, I was devastated. I almost didn't attend the scouting event.

I have no idea what the sermon was about that Sunday morning. Tears streamed down my face as I sat there staring at that picture of Jesus while God's Holy Spirit made some things very clear to me. He powerfully showed me that God, the Father, and Jesus, the Son, had loved each other even more than Grandma Myrtle and I had loved each other.

I was still in agony and grief caused by being separated from Grandma. Then I realized that God and Jesus, knowing the agony to come, had willingly been separated when Jesus died on the cross. It was very agonizing and excruciatingly painful for them both.

That's what Jesus was expressing in Matthew 27:46, *And about the ninth hour Jesus cried with a loud voice, saying, Eli, Eli, lama sabachthani? That is to say, My God, my God, why hast thou forsaken me?*

I was also made to understand that the reason God and Jesus had made such a huge and painful sacrifice was so that people could go to heaven. Years later I read in Hebrews 12:2 about how Jesus endured the cross, despising the shame, so that He could experience the joy of bringing us to the Father!

That morning in Port Townsend, I was made to know the truth even before I read the verses and my tears became tears of joy. I didn't even care that I was wearing shorts as I made my way back to the bus to return to the Girl Scout camp.

That revelation of God's tender and powerful love sustained me for years. Since my family rarely attended church, I didn't learn any more about God until I got to college seven years later.

During my freshman year at MSU in Bozeman, one fall afternoon, I heard the gospel of Jesus Christ. A Campus Crusade for Christ counselor, Shirley Peterson, met with me and led me through the Four Spiritual Laws booklet. I had never heard that we could invite Jesus into our hearts, or that He died to forgive us of all sin, so we could become God's born again children. I was eager to ask Him! I was born again that autumn afternoon in 1972.

What Jesus had done on the cross long ago, went from being history in my mind to being gospel (good news) in my life!

Marvel not that I said unto thee, Ye must be born again.
John 3:7

Easter Eggs

Easter was almost always a happy day in my childhood. My family usually had an Easter egg hunt. So, on Easter, I'd wake up full of joy, hope, and excitement about what I would find.

Unfortunately, most days while growing up, I'd wake up with fear and anxiety about what might happen in our anger explosive home. That fear and seriousness carried over into my college days, even though I lived in the dorm and not at home.

However, the first morning after I had invited Jesus Christ into my heart, I woke up in my dorm room with that same joy, hope, and excitement that I had experienced as a child on Easter morning. I loved that I belonged to God and I sensed that He would watch out for me, take good care of me, and lead me into wonderful ways.

I was experiencing the only scripture I knew, Psalms 23. *The Lord is my shepherd, I shall not want. . . Surely goodness and mercy shall follow me all the days of my life; and I will dwell in the house of the LORD forever.*

After 40 years, that buoyant joy has not departed. Amazingly, even during the most difficult times in my life, there was, deep in my spirit, an undeniably powerful joy. Most people that I meet notice my joy almost immediately. I'm not making the effort to be joyful, it just springs forth.

That joy continues to be fueled by such loving verses and promises such as the first one that God made "leap off" the page, Romans 8:28, *And we know that all things work together for good to them that love God, to them who are the called according to His purpose.*

Wow! God was going to work *everything* together for my good. What a promise! I also loved Romans 8:31, *What shall we then say to these things? If God be for us, who can be against us?*

Another verse that amazed me was Hebrews 13:5c, *for He hath said, I will never leave thee, nor forsake thee.*

Years later, while I was reading the Bible and seeking God, the Lord showed me that we give Him great pleasure by treating him as a loving parent who is continually setting out "Easter eggs" for His beloved children to find. He is the most wonderful parent in the world.

*These things have I spoken unto you, that my joy might remain in you
and that your joy might be full.*
John 15:11

You Let Me

I praise God that with childlike faith, since becoming a Believer in college, I have read the Bible and believed it was truth. Unfortunately, my parents didn't share my new found faith, but I hoped they would. So, I often told my parents what God had done for me as a result of a prayer or by making a verse from the Bible become so real and powerful in my life.

Once during a visit, while my parents were on campus, I excitedly told them about another good thing that God had done for me. In exasperation, my mother turned to me and said, "Oh, if God did everything you say He does for you, He wouldn't even have time to help anyone else!"

"Oh yes, He would," I confidently answered, "Because He is God."

I believe that quick, bold answer came straight from God. However, Mom's question got me to thinking. It did seem like I experienced God and His provisions much more often and stronger than many other Christians, even though I was a rather new Believer.

So, I prayed and asked God, "Why is it, dear Lord, that You show me so many things and You do so much for me? In Jesus' name."

His answer was swift and simple, "Because you let Me."

But without faith it is impossible to please Him: for he that cometh to God must believe that He is, and that He is a rewarder of them that diligently seek Him.
Hebrews 11:6

Lord of Lords

*F*or the first few months after inviting Jesus Christ into my heart, I loved to hear anyone talk about God, or Father, or Jesus, or Savior, or Redeemer, or Lamb of God. However, there was one name of God that didn't excite me. In fact, every time I heard someone use it, I almost shuddered and thought, "Oh, how *religious* that sounds."

I never used the title or name of Lord for God or Jesus. That was almost like fingernails on a chalkboard to me.

One afternoon, alone in my dorm room, I was thinking about that when I realized it was odd of me, since Lord is a name used in the Bible for both God and Jesus. LORD in all capitals usually refers to God, the Father, and Lord in lower case, usually refers to Jesus, the Son.

Then clearly the Holy Spirit spoke to my spirit and said, "The reason that you don't like the word Lord is because He is *not* Lord of your life."

Wow! Talk about conviction, it took my breath away. I fell to my knees beside my dorm bed. Then and there, I confessed that I had been so wrong, not to let Jesus be Lord of my life. Of course He deserved that title and position. I invited Him to be, not just Savior, but Lord of my life for the rest of my life.

I meant it. He knew it. He has truly reigned as Lord of my life from that day on. Since then, one of my favorite names for Jesus is Lord of lords and King of kings. I can't wait until He returns again as Revelation 19:16 says, *He hath on His vesture and on His thigh a name written, KING OF KINGS, AND LORD OF LORDS.*

I believe that sincere decision to make Jesus my Lord, is the main reason that I have had such a victorious, exciting life. I've devoured His Word and tried to be completely obedient. As a result, God has revealed to me how powerful, majestic, mighty, and glorious Jesus is. That's how I always think of Him, radiant with glory and power. Too many people think of him as meek, mild, emaciated, and weak. That is *not* the way He is.

Let's remember that Philippians 2:5-8 teaches us that Jesus was equal with God. It was with great love and courage, Jesus chose to make Himself of no reputation. He took the form of a servant man who humbled Himself to the shameful, painful death on the cross, in order to take our place. Of course, after all the torture and abuse, Jesus was exhausted, but He was not and is not weak!

In Matt. 26:53, after Judas had betrayed Him, Jesus said that He could ask for, and receive, over 12 legions of angels. Since a legion then was between 3,000 and 6,000 that would have been at least between 36,000 and 72,000 angels! Jesus had, and still has, mind boggling power!

It is imperative for us to understand and believe the power and majesty of our Lord Jesus Christ. All power has been given to Him, in heaven and in earth (Matthew 28:18). He upholds all things by the word of His power (Hebrew 1:3). He is seated at God Almighty's right hand (Acts 2:33-36).

These shall make war with the Lamb. And the Lamb shall overcome them: for He is Lord of lords, and King of kings: and they that are with Him are called, and chosen, and faithful.
Rev. 17:14

Unsigned Check

*J*esus said in John 14:13, *"And whatsoever ye shall ask in my name, that will I do, that the Father may be glorified in the Son."*

Those words made me believe it was Jesus' strong desire to answer prayer. So, when I prayed, I expected answers to my prayers because that's what Jesus wanted. Others weren't receiving answered prayer the way I was. So, I asked the Father, "Why?"

That's when He showed me the mental picture parable of the unsigned check. This parable explains many unanswered prayers.

When we ask for something in prayer, it's as if we are presenting a check to be cashed at the heavenly bank from Jesus' account. He is the One who opened the account by paying the price, even unto death, to make us joint heirs with Him (Romans 8:17).

He made us joint signers on the salvation account, which includes so much more than merely going to Heaven when we die. Salvation means complete wholeness, peace, lacking nothing. It is a very rich account!

So, we pray, or present our check, knowing that His account's abundantly sufficient (Philippians 4:19). However, if the check is unsigned, it doesn't have to be honored. Just so, when a prayer is made without asking "in Jesus' name," it's like a check that is unsigned. It doesn't have to be honored.

We must be sure that we are correctly presenting the check, or the prayer, in three ways. First, we must be asking for assets that are placed in the bank. In this case, praying for God's will as revealed by His Word and His Holy Spirit.

Secondly, we need to present the check to the bank, or expectantly ask the Lord with the confidence that His account, in this case, His Word, is trustworthy.

Lastly, we must present a *signed* check which is to ask in Jesus' holy name. That is not the same as asking "for His sake" or "for His glory." or just ending with "Amen."

Let's do what Jesus said and ask in His name. Then we will be bringing Him glory.

If ye shall ask anything in my name, I will do it.
John 14:14

Middle C

It is quite clear in Romans 8:29, God's good plan is for all of us to be conformed to the image of His dear Son, Jesus. So, as a young Believer, I assumed that if every Christian was closely following God and His will, then we would all become the same. It was frustrating and rather confusing to me that there were so many differences.

Furthermore, I felt condemnation when I didn't do some things as well as others. Or worse yet, I had pride and a sense of superiority when I did something better than another Christian. I knew that was definitely not part of God's good plan!

One afternoon, the Lord really taught me about His plan by showing me a music parable. He showed me that I had been thinking everyone should be made into a perfectly pitched, identically sounding Middle C note.

God clearly showed me that He was *not* at all interested in making everyone into a Middle C note. Rather, He wanted to create a beautiful symphony with many different notes.

He showed me that He would use high notes, low notes, loud notes, soft notes, even sharps and flats! Under His direction, we are each to become what He has created us to be. We are also to allow Him to place each of us in His symphony where and when He wants us. He will be the Composer and the Director, and the symphony will be beautiful, especially to Him!

That truth was wonderfully freeing to me. We each get to be what God created us to be. No more condemnation from others for my being different and no more pride towards other who are different from me.

Thou art worthy, O Lord, to receive glory and honor and power: for thou hast created all things, and for thy pleasure they are and were created.
Revelation 4:11

God's Jigsaw Puzzle

*Ha*ve you ever been working on a jigsaw puzzle and really trying hard to get some pieces to fit in, but you just seemed to be stumped? Then you decide to examine the picture on the box very closely. You'll see things that you hadn't noticed, or remembered. You'll understand the placement better and you can usually get some more of the jigsaw picture puzzle completed.

It's the same thing spiritually. We need to look closely at God's "picture on the box" to see what it is that He's trying to build into our lives. The ultimate picture is Jesus Christ. Remember God is transforming us into the image of His dear Son (Rom. 8:29).

That's where the Bible becomes an invaluable tool. We are dealing with a spiritual picture that is so much higher than the way we normally think (Isaiah 55:8). God's "picture" plan is so immeasurably more glorious than we have ever dared to understand. God the Father really does want to make us very much like Jesus! Let that glorious truth wash over you.

As we read the Bible, God will show us the "picture on the box" and instruct us in the ways of righteousness. His Word, revealed by His Spirit, does give us very practical, easy to understand guidelines, along with very personal specific details for whatever situation we might face.

Remember that you have an enemy of your soul who is dead set on destroying the picture God has for your life. The enemy will try to replace God's wonderful picture with cheap, selfish, greedy, or lazy pictures that result in sin, sickness, and heartbreak. The Bible helps you to understand whose picture you are beholding and therefore becoming.

You become what you behold. That is the strong message in II Corinthians 3:18, *But we all, with open face beholding as in a glass* [mirror] *the glory of the Lord, are changed into the same image from glory to glory, even as by the Spirit of the Lord.*

That verse is even clearer in the Amplified version. It says, *And all of us, as with unveiled face, [because we] continued to behold [in the Word of God] as in a mirror the glory of the Lord, are constantly being transfigured into His very own image in ever increasing splendor from one degree of glory to another; [for this comes] from the Lord [Who is] the Spirit.*

Jesus always trusted that His Father not only saw the "picture on the box," but also knew exactly what to do to bring it to completion in Jesus' life. That's why He always did and said whatever the Father wanted Him to do. Jesus didn't do anything except what the Father wanted Him to do (John 8:28).

Now when we read about that game plan of Jesus, we think, "Wow! Wouldn't that be great? I wish I could do that too."

Well, I am convinced that if we are willing to pay the price, if we really want God's "picture" for us, He will communicate clearly what the next piece is in the puzzle and what we are to do.

We also need to understand that sometimes a certain puzzle piece might look ugly, or painful, or boring. However, if it is from God, it is worth figuring out where that piece of the puzzle goes in our life.

Sometimes we have to be willing to endure the loneliness, the trials, and hardships to complete the glorious masterpiece. Never forget, God's "picture" for you is magnificent!

For I know the thoughts and plans that I have for you, says the Lord, thoughts and plans for welfare and peace and not for evil, to give you hope in your final outcome.
Jeremiah 29:11, Amplified Bible

Migraine Headaches Gone

*W*hile in high school, I started having excruciatingly painful migraine headaches. Each time, before the awful pain began, I would see bright points of lights in front of my eyes and be nauseated.

As a freshman in college, I hadn't had any migraines. I'd been a Christian Believer for a few months and I had been daily devouring the Bible. I loved reading the gospel stories filled with the healings and miracles that Jesus had done. I was also memorizing many Bible verses, because they were so incredible.

One particular day, I had just memorized Hebrews 13:8, *Jesus Christ, the same yesterday, and today, and forever.* That evening I went to the cafeteria for dinner. I was walking into the restroom when, all of a sudden, I saw the dreaded bright lights and felt the nausea begin.

I clutched the metal shelf that stuck out of the wall, above the sinks. I closed my eyes and from the bottom of my heart I cried out, "Dear God, please help me. I've been reading about all the healings that Jesus did so many times. Now I've just memorized the verse that says Jesus Christ is the same yesterday, today, and forever. I think that means that Jesus can heal today too. If that's true, would you please heal me from this migraine headache? In Jesus' name I pray. Amen and thank you."

The minute that I opened my eyes, the bright lights were gone and there was no more nausea. That same Jesus that I had been reading about in my Bible, had just healed me!

I've never had another migraine headache in my life, even though there were times that my score on the stress test was off the charts. I've also learned that guilt can cause migraines, and Jesus has freed me from that too.

I really learned a powerful lesson that day. Jesus Christ is still in the miracle working business! God was blazingly alive among the people in yesterday years, and I believe that He still wants to be blazingly alive in our lives today and tomorrow. Aren't you glad? I am.

And Jesus went about all Galilee, teaching in their synagogues, and preaching the gospel of the kingdom, and healing all manner of sickness and all manner of disease among the people.
Matthew 4:23

Holy Hunch

During our dating days in college, my fiancé, Leigh, and I were attending an afternoon party hosted by my dorm mother for all her resident advisors of Hapner Hall at Montana State University. We were at her beautiful home situated in the woods near Red Lodge, Montana.

During the day, Leigh did something that hurt me, but he didn't want to discuss it. So I went outside to be alone with God in the beautiful autumn sun. As I walked along the road, I was praying to God. Then I wandered a short distance into the thick trees, well out of sight of the house.

I was praying to God about what had happened and praying that for once in our 3 years of dating, Leigh would take the initiative to make things right, rather than just ignore the issue, carry on as usual, and wait for me to be the one to come up with the ideas for reconciliation.

As I poured my heart out to God, a very wonderful sense of peace and compassion surrounded me like a warm blanket. Then a hunch, or very strong impression came to me, to go back to a certain place in the road.

At first, I just wanted to stay in the beautiful spot I'd found, surrounded by God's loving presence. The urging continued, so I headed to the indicated place.

There was Leigh! He was looking for me and about to give up, not having any idea where in the woods I might be. He had been acting on a hunch also. We joyfully ran to each other, hugged, made up, and discovered that God can use holy hunches to direct us.

And thine ears shall hear a word behind thee, saying, This is the way, walk
ye in it, when ye turn to the right hand, and when ye turn to the left.
Isaiah 30:21

V-8 Moment

*Sh*ortly after becoming a born again Believer in Jesus Christ, I realized that I would one day stand in His presence. That is made quite clear in II Corinthians 5:10, *For we must all appear before the judgment seat of Christ, that everyone may receive the things done in his body, according to what he hath done, whether it be good or bad.*

I praise God for helping me understand that when I actually behold Him in all His glory and power, I do *not* want to hit my forehead like the popular V-8 commercial. Remember where the person chose to drink something else and then realized that they could have had a V-8, so they hit their own head with remorse?

I do think that it would be a HUGE mistake to live my life as a Christian Believer acting as if God was a weak untrustworthy being who couldn't possibly mean what the Bible says. Then after having lived such a meager cowardly life, to actually behold the Glorious One!

I would realize, "Oh, if I had only known what You were really like, I would have lived my life totally different! I would have done what You said." What a grief that would be to God and to me.

So, very early in my walk with God, I determined to get to know Him, as well as I possibly could. I decided *not* make the mistakes of underestimating Him or not really living my life the way He wanted. That was one of the best decisions that I've ever made. My passion for over 40 years has been to know our great God, to know His ways, and to live them.

The knowledge of the Holy One has given me great courage and a desire to help others to know God as He really is, and *not* to settle for some watered down, weak version of the real thing! What a wonderful difference the body of Christ would be making if we all really obeyed the instructions of Hebrews 3:1, *Wherefore, holy brethren, partakers of the heavenly calling, consider the Apostle and High Priest of our profession, Christ Jesus.*

This is how Webster defines consider: "to look at carefully, to think or deliberate on, with a view to action, to show regard for, to believe." Isn't it interesting that the Bible does *not* tell us to consider the obstacles we face, nor to consider that others say it can't be, but rather, to consider Christ Jesus. We would do very well to actually consider Jesus.

It's fantastic that as we seek to know Him better, to understand His ways more clearly, and to walk in them, He reveals more to us. That's what Jesus was teaching in Matthew 13:11-12, [Jesus]...*said unto them, Because it is given unto you to know the mysteries of the kingdom of heaven, but to them it is not given. For whosoever has* [spiritual knowledge] *to him shall be given, and he shall have more abundance; but whosoever hath not, from him shall be taken away even what he hath.*

I've heard it said, and I believe it's true, that we will have as much of God as we want. He longs for us to know Him, but He is not interested in being a cheap, thrill seeking experience for anyone. He wants our whole heart before He reveals the depths of His heart. That's what He tells us in Jeremiah 29:13, *And ye shall seek Me, and find Me, when ye shall search for Me with all your heart.*

He deserves our utmost reverential awe, or fear. That is the attitude that invites God to reveal Himself to us.

The secret of the LORD is with those who fear Him; and He will show them His covenant.
Psalms 25:14

In the Lake

A puzzling scripture to me, as a new Believer, was John 14:20. Jesus says, *"At that day you shall know that I am in my Father, and you in me, and I in you."*

How could we both be inside? How could I be in Jesus, and Jesus be in me? In my logical mind, it seemed that someone had to be in the inside and someone had to be on the outside. I was thinking on this and waiting for God to show me the truth.

He presented this simple picture in my mind. There I was standing, waist-deep, in a beautiful, crystal clear lake. So I was inside the lake. Then, I saw myself, while still standing in the lake, scoop up some water and drink it. Now the water was inside me.

I understood that I was in Jesus Christ, as a Believer in Him. There are many verses in the Bible that talk about us being in Christ. One of my favorite is II Corinthians 5:17. It teaches us, *"Therefore if any man* [or woman] *be in Christ, let him be a new creature; old things are passed away; behold, all things are become new."*

At the same time that I was in Jesus, He would be in me, by His Spirit, especially as I let His Word dwell richly in me according to Colossians 3:16a, *"Let the word of Christ dwell in you richly in all wisdom."*

I think II Corinthians 1:21-22 shows the situation quite well and explains that it is God doing both things in our lives. *"Now He who established us with you in Christ, and has anointed us, is God; Who has also sealed us, and given the earnest of the Spirit in our hearts."*

Abide in me, and I in you. As the branch cannot bear fruit of itself, except
it abide in the vine; no more can you, except you abide in me.
John 15:4

Kitchen Barstool

During college, summertime dating meant Leigh and I saw each other only a couple of weekends a month, when my family drove to our A-frame cabin near Holland Lake, Montana. Leigh spent his summer days in nearby Condon, helping his Grandma Minnie and her husband, Andy. They owned the local gas station/store. Evenings he'd visit my family.

In June, 1974, Leigh decided it would be great to make a kitchen barstool for me. He proudly designed it with a variety of woods. He carefully turned the legs and rungs on his late grandfather's lathe. Leigh diligently spent hours proudly and carefully building, sanding, and varnishing that barstool.

One Friday evening my family arrived at the cabin and, as usual, Leigh came to dinner. He decided to leave early because he wanted to put on another layer of varnish. We walked to his car together. He left.

I stayed outside with my aching heart. Leaning against the cabin, I blinked back tears as I looked up into the night sky. I hurt.

Softly I cried out, "Dear God, I don't want to be ungrateful that Leigh is making me a gift and working so hard to make it beautiful. But all I really want is for Leigh to be with me, to love me, and to spend some time with me. I've missed him. Please help me to have the right attitude, in Jesus' name. Amen."

I expected God to deal with me about being ungrateful. I was willing for Him to correct me, change my heart, and please help the pain go away.

Instead He surprised me by gently speaking into my spirit. "I understand exactly how you feel. I long for my people to be with Me, to love Me, and to spend time with Me. Instead they're busy doing things that they think they're doing to please Me. I completely understand your pain."

Wow! While gazing at towering ponderosa pines through my tears, I realized the pain that God suffers when His people are too busy to be still and know Him. I decided that I would *not* do that to Him.

He had shown me that the best gift I could ever give Him was my love. I determined to be at least one person on earth who loves Him dearly, and to always let that be my main focus.

Sacrifice and offering thou didst not desire; mine ears hast thou opened;
Then said I, Lo, I come.
Psalms 40:6a, 7a

Speed Boats

As a freshman in college when I invited Jesus Christ into my heart, I was like a dry sponge soaking up God's great love into my life. I yearned to know this wonderful God of love. I had been studying the Bible with a campus group that was eager to introduce people to Jesus Christ as their Savior, but, they taught that we didn't get any more of God's Holy Spirit than we received when we were born again. They also taught that it was not of God to speak in tongues, and was wrong to do so. I believed them.

I was also going to another Bible study in the dorm. That leader was the only person who did admit to me that she spoke in tongues and felt it was very valuable. From what I could tell, she was godlier, more in love with God, and she understood God better than anyone else I knew.

She loaned me a copy of Nine O'clock in the Morning by Dennis J. Bennett. Reading that and checking the accompanying Bible verses helped me to see what the Bible says about being filled with the Holy Spirit.

I wanted to obey God and be all that He wanted me to be. However, I was rather hesitant to pursue something so openly opposed by the group who had led me to God. I was very confused, but I believed that God would teach me whatever I needed to know.

So, I got down on my knees beside my dorm bed and prayed to my Heavenly Father, "If You want me to pray in tongues I will, if You don't, I won't, in Jesus' name. Amen."

Nothing happened except that I had a real peace knowing I was totally surrendered to whatever God wanted. I knew that I could trust Him.

Several months later, during a trying time with some very demanding people, I went into a room to be by myself and to pray for strength from my Abba (Daddy) God. All of a sudden, different sounds were coming out of my mouth. It almost sounded like, "La, la, la."

I was filled with new joy and new strength. I had just been filled with the Holy Spirit in a new way, like described in Acts!

I also discovered that after that experience, whenever I read the Bible, it was so much clearer, more real, and very powerful. I wasn't just reading about other people being at the foot of Jesus listening to Him. It was as if I was right there, at His feet, listening too. I also realized that when I was praying in that language, there was a very strong sense that the enemy was fleeing.

Then the Lord showed me a picture parable about all this. I saw a wide rushing river that represented life. It was flowing rapidly towards a huge crashing waterfall that would be deadly to go over.

Every person on earth was in a small rowboat and had two oars. Some were rowing diligently, trying with all their might to row upstream, to avoid going over the waterfall. Many others, ignoring the waterfall, weren't even using their oars except to play and splash other rowboats.

When people got saved and born again, God lifted them out of the rowboats and placed each person in a speed boat. Then He showed me something that was startling. Many of the people in the speed boats were still using their two oars to try to navigate their speed boat!

Needless to say, they weren't making much progress against the mighty river. In fact, many seemed to be losing ground and getting closer to the waterfall. They were exhausted and very discouraged.

Then God showed me that when we are baptized in the Holy Spirit, it is like getting a motor on our speed boat. With motors, the speed boats can easily navigate up the river without becoming exhausted.

We are empowered by Him to live the life that He desires for us. Our lives will show *Thy kingdom come, Thy will be done in earth, as it is in Heaven* (Matthew 6:10).

Becoming a child of God is so much more than simply agreeing to a creed and joining a church. Many clubs, organizations, and some churches exist on those principles. Some clubs form to do good works and provide a social place for their members to belong. That can be fine and good, but becoming a child of God involves an encounter with the supernatural God.

This experience is described in I Peter 1:23, *Being born again, not of corruptible seed, but of incorruptible, by the word of God, which liveth and abideth forever.*

It is a new experience and it changes us. That's why II Corinthians 5:17 says, *"Therefore if any man be in Christ, he is a new creature; old things are passed away; behold, all things are become new."*

If you're still trying to navigate through life just using your own devices, or oars, I invite you to discover the mighty way of God's Holy Spirit.

These [mockers] *are they who separate themselves, sensual, having not the Spirit. But ye, beloved, building up yourselves on your most holy faith, praying in the Holy Ghost, keep yourselves in the love of God, looking for the mercy of our Lord Jesus Christ unto eternal life.*
Jude 1:19-21

Dazzling Diamond

I was enjoying the benefits of being filled with God's Holy Spirit. God was even closer to me than before. The Bible was so much more alive and powerful. Praying had a supernatural strength to it. I was very aware that God was doing mighty things in my life.

Then I had a new question for God, "How come since this is such a wonderful, uplifting, strengthening thing, (Jude 1:20), why don't all Christians teach that it is a good thing and encourage everyone to experience it? In Jesus' name, Amen."

He answered me so clearly that I can still remember it over 40 years later. He brought a picture of a HUGE dazzling diamond to my mind. Then He revealed to me that He was like that diamond. Each face on the diamond represented a facet of Him. Each facet was true, such as Father, Savior, Comforter, Healer, Baptizer, and so many more.

The Lord also made me to know that some people will discover some facet about God and then they fearfully refuse to view anymore facets of God. They are afraid that discovering another facet of Him negates the truth of the earlier facets.

In that wonderful moment, God revealed that it would take a lifetime, or more correctly, eternity, to get to know all the facets of Him. He also made me to know that His children never need to be afraid of learning more about God.

Of course we must try the spirits whether they are of God (I John 4:1). We must also look for confirmation in the Bible.

That was the day in my life that I made the quality decision to spend the rest of my life getting to know God in as many of His facets as I possibly could. It has been a glorious discovery that does not end!

I am the Alpha and Omega, the beginning and the ending, saith the Lord, who is, and who was, and who is to come, the Almighty.
Revelation 1:8

Powerful Praise

I don't even remember when I first said, "Praise the Lord!"

It was just the perfect expression of what I was feeling and experiencing. I really was in awe of God. I was delighted with what wonderful things that He was doing in my life and all around me. It still is my favorite expression for those very same reasons.

As a new Believer, I read Psalms 42:11, *Why art thou cast down, O my soul? And why art thou disquieted* [upset] *within me? Hope thou in God, for I shall yet praise Him, who is the health of my countenance* [face], *and my God.*

When I read that verse I realized that my part was to praise God and His part was to keep my face healthy. We've both kept our part of the deal. I have the easy part, praising Him all day long for Who He is and what He does.

I love and praise Him that He never leaves me or forsakes me (Hebrews 13:5). I praise Him for answered prayer. I praise Him for creation and beauty. I praise Him for communicating with me. I praise Him for giving me good ideas. I praise Him for my family and friends. I praise Him for keeping His Word. I praise Him for being so loving. I praise Him for being so strong and protecting, and yet so gentle with His children. I could go on and on, but you get the idea. I praise Him with a thankful heart all day long.

He has kept my face healthy and youthful. When I began substitute teaching at the high school, I was 29 years old, yet, several of the teachers thought I was a new student! When I was 52, I'd be mistaken for my 28 year old son's date. Nowadays, most people are surprised to learn that I am 60. I realize that since God has given me eternal life, these years are just a drop in the eternal bucket of time.

I appreciate that He has renewed me, just like Isaiah 40:31 says, *They that wait upon the LORD shall renew their strength; they shall mount up with wings as eagles; they shall run, and not be weary; and they shall walk and not faint.*

The greatest blessing of praise is that He inhabits the praises of His people (Psalms 22:3). So I praise Him and play praise music as much as possible to invite Him to be with me, and to constantly give Him the glory He deserves.

I will praise thee, O Lord my God, with all my heart: and I will glorify thy name for evermore.
Psalms 86:12

White Stallion

About two years after I had invited Jesus into my heart, my husband and I were back at college as newlyweds and I was absolutely exhausted. All my type A, perfectionist life, I had pushed myself to be and do my best at whatever I did. Now that I was a Christian and a new wife, I certainly could do no less.

I was striving to get straight A's while taking 22-24 college credits each trimester, so that I could get a 4 year degree in 3 years. I was attending and/or leading three different Bible studies every week, one as early as 5 am. I was also trying to be all that my husband wanted me to be, while dealing with a marriage that was extremely difficult.

One evening, after an invitation to another Christian leadership meeting, I went into the bathroom and I sank to my knees in weary tears. I told God that I loved Him so much but that I was so tired of trying to do everything. I just wanted to spend more time loving Him and not be doing anything more for a while, if it would be OK.

He clearly and gently spoke to my spirit, "Loving me *is* the most important thing that you can ever do," (Mark 12:29-30).

To make His point unforgettable, God also showed me another picture parable. I was frantically galloping atop a magnificent, strong, white stallion. God revealed to me that becoming a Christian can be like mounting a remarkable stallion.

The enemy will try his best to keep us from getting on that stallion. First, he lies that it will be a boring ride, or that nobody rides any more. If we do get on the stallion, or accept Jesus Christ as our savior, the enemy will push and pull every which way to try to get us to fall off the magnificent stallion, or live defeated, discouraged lives of shame.

What God revealed next was amazing and so helpful. I saw that when the enemy comes across someone who will not be kept off the stallion, nor pushed off the stallion, the enemy uses another tactic. He deceives us into thinking that we must gallop continuously to be a good rider, or a real Christian. We can literally exhaust ourselves. I certainly had. In fact, looking back, I think I was on the verge of a nervous breakdown.

Praise God for impressing upon me a truly life-changing revelation! Jesus is like the stallion. Our job is to simply get on the stallion, hang on for dear life, and then let the *stallion* choose when to gallop, when to trot, and when to be still.

As Believers, we must continually seek to be in Christ Jesus and to let Him set the pace and the direction for our lives. We are secure in Him (Colossians 2:9-10). We can let God be God. No more straining to be perfect, but rather we can surrender to the Perfect One and let Him live His life through us. We can be peaceful, no longer striving in our own strength.

I have never forgotten that lesson. It saved my mental health. It taught me to say "no" when it was necessary and to not feel guilty. It also helped me to be aware of how easy it can be to become so involved in the work of the Lord, that we leave the Lord of the work out of it. I never wanted to do that again, and by His grace, I haven't.

I do know deep inside that the most important thing that I will ever do is to love God, really love Him, with all my heart and mind and soul and strength. I do and I don't feel guilty about that, even when the Stallion is at rest.

Are you tired? Worn out? Burned out on religion? Come to me. Get away with me and you'll recover your life. I'll show you how to take a real rest. Walk with me and work with me—watch how I do it. Learn the unforced rhythms of grace.
Matthew 11:28-29, The Message Bible

Don't Rob God

*D*id you know that there is one place in the Bible that God almost dares us to trust Him? It's in the last book of the Old Testament, Malachi 3:10. *Bring all the tithes into the storehouse, that there may be food in mine house, and **test me now** herewith, saith the LORD of hosts, if I will not open for you the windows of heaven, and pour out for you a blessing, that there shall not be room enough to receive it.*

When I read that, as a new Believer, it was quite clear that God wanted me to give 10% of my income to His work and He was committing Himself to bless me and pour out more than enough for me. In other words, He would make my 90% go further than it would have, if I had kept it all for myself. He has indeed done that time and time again!

Not only that, but in the proceeding verses, Malachi 3:8-9, it's explained that if we did not tithe, we were robbing God and would be under a curse! *Will a man rob God? Yet you have robbed me. But you say, How have we robbed thee? In tithes and offerings. You are cursed with a curse; for you have robbed me, even this whole nation.*

As you can see, it doesn't matter if that's the way everyone is handling their money. It's still wrong and insulting to God, and He doesn't ignore it!

I was convinced that tithing was very important and determined to do it. I asked my fiancé, Leigh, and he agreed we'd tithe our money after we were married. I wouldn't have married him if he hadn't wanted to tithe.

We didn't start out with very much when we were married in 1974. We had a 1964 Studebaker car and the earnings from our summer jobs to pay for our next year of college tuition. We also had a jelly jar of Canadian coins that his parents had saved over the summer at their small gas station/convenience store in Montana. We took that on our Canadian honeymoon.

We have faithfully tithed for 40 years and we NEVER went without anything that we needed. We could always afford food, clothing, gas, or even a plane ticket to go where we wanted, no matter the price.

I was very thankful for that many years later when our son was going to college in Indiana. We were always able to get airline tickets for Adam to fly home for holidays and vacations, even while we were paying cash for his college.

When God Almighty opens windows of heaven to pour out blessings, like He promises in Malachi 3:10, He is not stingy! Of course we weren't wasteful, lazy, or extravagant. We also followed the Biblical principle to stay out of debt (Romans 13:8).

I remember one of my first grocery shopping trips early in our marriage. I saw meat that I wanted to buy, but God clearly said, "No."

At first I thought He didn't want me to have it. That was OK. I trusted that He knew best. Later, at another store, I saw the same item for quite a bit less per pound and He joyfully said, "Buy it here!"

Because of His presence and guidance, shopping for food, clothing, cars, gifts, or anything has been a special time that I've had with the Lord. I let Him guide me as to what, where, and when to buy. Of course, we have a budget, I read ads, and make shopping lists, but He always has the final say in all my purchases.

When Adam and Rebekah were toddlers, we taught them to tithe too. We had a colorful little piggybank in the shape of a church. When they got their small allowances, the first thing they'd do was put 10% in the little church bank and we called it "God's money." Today they both make excellent incomes and they still give "God's money" to Him. I am so proud of them, and they are both blessed mightily in their finances!

I have also been blessed financially beyond my wildest dreams. Not only do we live in a dream house that I designed. We even have an indoor swimming pool. I had always hoped to visit Hawaii some day and now we even have a time share condo there. I could probably write an entire book about His financial blessings to us.

Whoever despises the word and counsel [of God] brings destruction upon himself, but he who [reverently] fears and respects the commandment [of God] is rewarded.
Proverbs 13:13, Amplified Bible

Radio Warning

*O*ur first summer as newlyweds, in 1975, Leigh and I lived in a one room kitchenette motel facing the highway on the outskirts of Worland, Wyoming, a small agricultural town. We were there because Leigh was interning as an agricultural engineer and there was nowhere else to rent. He often travelled out of town and spent nights away each week for that job.

Although we made some wonderful friends that summer from the church we attended, I usually spent the days and nights alone in the motel room reading, sewing, cooking, and writing letters. I almost always had the little electric clock-radio tuned to a Christian station that played wonderful praise music and offered good Bible teaching. The radio reception was sometimes sketchy, but one day God used that radio to save me from grave danger!

The story actually begins the night before. We were renting the end unit of the motel, and hadn't had a neighbor very often. I'd never noticed any noise from neighbors. Leigh and I had made love that night in the bed which was close to the wall, not realizing that the walls of the motel were probably rather thin.

The next morning the construction worker from next door came out to get into his truck while I was giving Leigh a goodbye kiss and hug at our front door The man sneered at me with such a lustful dirty look, it made me shiver.

I was wearing my red and white thick furry knee length bathrobe that tied at my waist. There was *nothing* indecent or immodest about it.

Leigh was going to be gone for a few days and nights. So, I was just contentedly working in the motel and listening to the little radio that afternoon.

All of a sudden there was loud static over the radio and I heard two men talking, maybe on CB radios. It was *not* from the radio station!

The first man asked the other man if he wanted to go somewhere. His answer was, "Nope, I'm heading back to the wenchy wench in the Santa Claus."

Immediately the Holy Spirit made me to know that I had just heard our motel neighbor talking and he was referring to me! Then God urged me, "Hurry! Get a few things together and get out of here! Go to Hartley's. Hurry!"

Hartleys were one of the kind families that we had met at the church. I hoped they would welcome me. I was so frightened that I was literally shaking while I threw together a few toiletries, my Bible, and some clothes. I usually over-pack, trying to be prepared. Not that time.

God urged me to "Hurry!" several times. I did.

Just as I was just putting my car in reverse to leave the motel parking lot, right outside our front door, the worker drove up beside me in his pickup. He was furious! He was mouthing some words at me and glaring at me. My windows were up and my doors were locked. I drove to my friend's home and stayed there until Leigh came back to town. By then the workers had moved on.

That radio never intercepted any other CB messages all summer. Praise God for protecting me!

And the Lord shall deliver me from every evil work, and will preserve me unto His heavenly kingdom: to whom be glory for ever and ever Amen.
II Timothy 4:18

Awesome Angel

When we graduated from Montana State University, my husband, Leigh, accepted an engineering position in Worland, Wyoming. We lived in that small agricultural town for about three years. Most of the time, it was a peaceful community.

However, there was one time when I was very frightened. I don't even remember the nature of the crimes, except that I'd become very scared to be alone overnight in our rented mobile home while Leigh was out on his extensive road trips with his new job. He'd often leave on Mondays and return on Fridays. That was in the days before we had cell phones.

I did what I always do when there is a problem—I turned to God.

One night as I was praying about my feelings of fear and asking Him to protect me, He showed me a vision of an angel standing in my backyard, near my bedroom window.

Up to that time, in various art forms, I had seen little chubby figures of angels and pictures of rather feminine featured angels with long flowing robes. The angel that stood in my backyard was nothing like any of those angels!

This angel looked more like the trademark giant of Mr. Clean. He was huge, at least 7 feet tall. He was very masculine with bulging muscles. He stood with his feet planted slightly apart and his arms were folded across his chest. The look on his face was one of absolute confidence and I knew that his mission was to protect me.

All feelings of fear vanished. I rested peacefully in my Heavenly Father's wonderful care, so thankful for the strong angel He had sent to guard me.

Bless the LORD, ye His angels, that excel in strength, that do His commandments, hearkening unto the voice of His word.
Psalms 103:20

Popcorn Canister

As a new Christian, I had a great desire to read the Bible, and the wonderful thing is that after forty-plus years, that desire still remains. This true story illustrates one of the reasons that I love God's Word.

Whenever I read something in the Bible that doesn't make sense to me, I simply ask God to please show me what this really means. Then I fully expect Him to do just that, one way or another.

This is how He taught me the meaning of Jesus' words in Luke 6:38, *"Give and it shall be given unto you; good measure, pressed down, and shaken together, and running over, shall men give unto your bosom. For with the same measure that ye measure it shall be measured to you again."*

I had a mental impression of something being so tightly packed together it seemed smashed, crunched, and maybe even broken in the process of being delivered to me. Yet, I could tell that Jesus was talking about something that was supposed to be good, so I just asked Him to please show me the truth.

Months later, after we had moved to Worland, Wyoming, I was in the kitchen pouring popcorn from the huge, value-priced bag into the cute canister. I really wanted to get all the popcorn into the canister so I could toss the bag rather than find space for it in the small kitchen.

Even though the canister looked full, I kept pouring kernels in. I was tapping the sides and shaking the canister. I even lightly banged the canister on the kitchen counter so the popcorn would settle and make room for a few more kernels.

As I was doing that, it was as if the Holy Spirit cleared His throat and said, "Ahem, this is what good measure pressed down, shaken together means. It is completely filled to the brim, as full as possible, and not broken, but in excellent shape."

I get it, Lord, thank You!

But the Comforter, who is the Holy Spirit, whom the Father will send in my name, He shall teach you all things, and bring all things to your remembrance, whatever I have said unto you.
John 14:26

More Tithing Blessings

*H*ave you noticed how you can read something in the Bible that you've read before, and then it becomes so clear that you wonder how you missed it earlier? That's because it is a living word, inspired by God just as II Timothy 3:16a states, *"All scripture is given by inspiration of God."*

The Holy Spirit of God can direct us to just what we need, when we need it. That's what He did one afternoon, in 1976, when we were living in Worland, Wyoming. We were renting a nice, clean mobile home situated on a small corner lot surrounded by other mobile homes. About half of our backyard was a vegetable garden. It was our first garden and it was a labor of love. We'd even done like the Pilgrims and placed a dead fish in with our corn seeds.

Our neighbors were a dear elderly couple, Ollie and Flora, who had recently become Christians. They were very eager to learn more about God and the Bible. In fact the first day that I met them, they invited me to a Bible study being taught in their home. I went gladly. When we finished, Ollie announced that I should teach the next one, which I did.

Ollie and Flora had such big hearts. They had converted their *entire* lot into a vegetable garden and they gave away most of what they grew!

It was late summer. Hail was predicted. I was very concerned for our many plants which weren't quite ready for harvest. Praying for guidance, I opened my Bible. It opened at Malachi 3:10, the tithing instructions. I read the next verse and wondered how had I missed it before?

Malachi 3:11 continues to tell of the blessings that God will do for the tither, *"And I will rebuke the devourer for your sakes, and he shall not destroy the fruits of your ground; neither shall your vine cast its fruit before the time in the field, saith the LORD of hosts."*

Later, hail began falling from the dark sky. In our garden, while the wind whipped my long hair into my upturned face, I prayed "Oh Lord, I've just read in Your Word that because we tithe, You will rebuke the devourer and he shall NOT destroy the fruits of our ground. I believe You, Lord, and ask You to do that for us now. I don't know if Ollie and Flora tithe or not, but would You please save their garden too? In Jesus' holy name. Amen."

Praise the Lord! Our garden was not damaged, and neither was Ollie and Flora's garden, even though others around us did have extensive damage in their yards and gardens from the hail. God is so mighty to honor His Word to us when we believe and obey.

If you know these things, happy are you if you do them.
John 13:17

God's Love Letters

One day while I was reading the Bible, God showed me a parable of someone pouring over a love letter. That person was enjoying each line and rereading the tender message over and over again.

Then the Lord showed me a picture of someone glancing at junk mail and tossing it aside. There was such a stark contrast to the first reader who was really valuing and enjoying what was being read.

God's next words amazed me, "That's the way people treat My Word, either as a love letter or as junk mail. For those to whom it is a love letter, there is great reward."

Wow! God had just personally verified Hebrews 11:6 to me. *"But without faith it is impossible to please Him: for he that cometh to God must believe that He is, and that He is a rewarder of them that diligently seek Him."*

My Grandpa Nellie gave me a KJV Bible with gold edged pages when I graduated from high school. That is one of the many Bibles that I have worn out from reading so much. I like to think that the gold is off the edges of the tattered pages and instead it's now in my heart.

I've read and memorized more from the King James Version Bible than any other version, and I have worn out a couple more KJVs since my Grandpa's gift. The Amplified Bible is another favorite version of mine. I also love reading the Message version. NavPress has stood behind their lifetime guarantee and sent me replacements when I've worn out Message Bibles from reading them so much. Isn't that a generous thing that they do? The Passion Translation is the newest version that I love!

I have probably read the Bible from cover to cover 50 or 60 times. I've read the New Testament well over 100 times. I've been to countless Bible studies and still love to listen to good Bible teachers. Mostly, I have opened His Word as a direct communication from the Most High God who loves me! Many times after reading just a verse or two, I simply pause to behold and enjoy the loving, powerful presence of God.

Reading the Bible isn't a duty for me. It's time spent with the Lover of my soul. The Bible is like a treasure map, but I think above all else, the Bible has always been a love letter to me. It's also my instruction manual. Since the instructions were inspired by the One who loves me so profoundly, how could I choose any other way?

Blessed art thou, O LORD: teach me thy statues. And I will delight myself in thy commandments, which I have loved.
Psalms 119:12 & 47

Delivering Donkey

Three years after our marriage we moved from Worland, Wyoming to a very small town in southwestern Wyoming. My husband, Leigh, had just taken a promotion as a field agricultural engineer. We didn't know anyone there and our families were back in Montana.

I was three months pregnant and eagerly awaiting the birth of our first child. Before we moved I had learned that there was only one physician in our new small town. After the move, I was very shocked to learn that he had moved to this town after a malpractice suit in another city involving a baby's death in childbirth.

Almost every pregnant woman from this small town went to Rock Springs, Wyoming, 75 miles away, or made the 135 mile trip to Salt Lake City, Utah to have their babies. I had a serious problem with that plan. I would probably have to drive myself to the doctor when the time came to deliver the baby. Our town was at 7000' elevation and only had 30 frost-free days. The baby was due December 29, 1977. I didn't want to have to be driving myself over icy mountain roads during my labor!

Since Leigh's job covered a huge L-shaped area of the state, he was out of town several nights during the week. Some weeks, he would leave on Monday morning and not return until Friday afternoon. Since much of his time was on the road or in the field, and cell phones were unheard of in those days, we usually only made contact at night. He'd call me from his hotel room. Leigh would try to be home for the baby's birth, but there was no guarantee.

As the weeks went by, I was becoming very distraught. I was taking the prenatal pills and following the advice of my previous doctor, but I knew that soon I should choose a doctor to be in charge of this birth. I was afraid to select an out of town doctor, because I didn't want to drive myself on icy winter mountain roads to the delivery room in another town or state. I was equally afraid to go to the only local doctor, because of the history.

Finally, I realized that it was time to be still and know God's perfect will for my life. As I was earnestly praying to God and utterly surrendering my life and my unborn baby's life into God's perfect will, He spoke to my spirit.

He asked me, "Do you trust me?"

I truthfully answered, "Yes, Lord."

He replied, "Then keep trusting me. Do not put your trust in men. Realize that I am the one in charge. I will be the one in charge of your baby's birth and I could make even a donkey deliver that baby, if it was necessary."

Such peace swept over me as joyful tears ran down my face. After laughing and celebrating with God for His wonderful goodness, I called the local doctor and made a prenatal appointment. The doctor was a gentle, kind man who did just fine.

Leigh and I took childbirth classes together and Leigh was in town to drive me to the local hospital. I knew that pain in childbirth was part of the curse (Genesis 3:16). I also knew that Jesus Christ had redeemed me from the curse of the law, being made a curse for us (Galatians 3:13). So, I went into the delivery expecting to be blessed and to not need drugs to cope with great pangs of pain. I didn't want any drugs to harmfully affect the baby. God's Word worked there too.

In the early hours of a January morning, our son, Adam, was born. It was a safe birth, without any drugs or complications.

Since it was such a tiny town, Adam was the first baby of 1978! "Adam Leigh Nelson a Winner" was the front page headline of the weekly newspaper. Adam's picture, with his eyes shut tightly, was on the front page too.

The newspaper photographer came to the hospital to take our photo with his camera that had a light twice the size of Adam's head. He kept asking me, "Isn't that baby going to open his eyes?"

I answered, "I don't think so," while I was earnestly praying under my breath that Adam wouldn't open his eyes and have the bright flash be so blinding. Finally the photo was taken, headlines were made, and we received many gifts from the local merchants. All this because I trusted God.to be in charge of delivering my baby.

It is better to trust in the LORD than to put confidence in man.
Psalms 118:8

Those Eyes

In the winter of 1978, when our firstborn, Adam, was only a few weeks old, the doctor diagnosed him with respiratory problems that could develop into pneumonia. On a Friday, the doctor told me that if there was no improvement very soon, Adam would have to be hospitalized.

My protective maternal instincts did not want my nursing newborn placed in the hospital. So I spent that night rocking Adam in a very steamy nursery while we listened to praise music. I prayed and meditated on all the verses that I could remember about Jesus healing people. I was really fighting a battle of fear and trying desperately to hear from God.

Sometime during that night, the Lord showed me a vision that profoundly changed my life and my family's lives forever. I saw Jesus Christ being whipped just before they crucified Him. His back was a bloody mess of slashes caused by the whip. Jesus was looking down. Then the vision zoomed in, just inches away from Jesus' head. He looked up, directly into my eyes. He spoke not a word with His lips, but oh, those eyes!

I saw such courage and strength and pain as His dark eyes penetrated into my very being. Without saying a word, Jesus Christ clearly communicated to me through His eyes, "If you do not receive healing because of these stripes, then this whipping was in vain."

That was mind boggling to me. Then I understood.

At the last supper, before He went to the cross, Jesus gave the cup of wine to His disciples. Then He said, *"For this is my blood of the new testament, which is shed for many for the remission of sins,"* (Matthew 26:28).

Many people understand that the blood of Jesus, the sinless Son of God, *had* to be shed for any of us to get forgiveness. Leviticus 17:11 strongly declares, *"For the life of the flesh is in the blood: and I have given it to you upon the altar to make an atonement* [reconciliation] *for your souls: for it is the blood that maketh an atonement for the soul."*

It is definitely true that without the shedding of Jesus' blood, there would have been no forgiveness for any of us. But so many people don't stop to realize that Jesus shed enough blood for our forgiveness from His hands and feet where the nails pierced Him, or from His side, when the spear gored Him. He let His back be whipped into a bloody mess of stripes so that we could be healed!

That's exactly what Isaiah the prophet was declaring about Jesus in Isaiah 53:5, *He was wounded for our transgressions, He was bruised for our iniquities; the chastisement of our peace was upon Him,* **and with His stripes we are healed.**

In a moment the vision disappeared, but the impact has remained for a lifetime. At that moment I knew that such suffering by Jesus Christ would *not* be in vain as far as I was concerned.

I rebuked the illness in Jesus name. I praised Jesus for what He had done for us. Adam improved dramatically and began breathing normally. We both slept peacefully the remainder of the night.

On Monday we went to a pediatric specialist in Salt Lake City, who stated, "This baby is just fine and has no need of these drugs anymore."

My family has lived in divine health ever since that night. We know that Jesus Christ has completely paid a huge price for our healing and we choose not to let that be in vain. We believe Isaiah 53:5. That truth is repeated in the New Testament too, in I Peter 2:24.

Who His own self bore our sins in His own body on the tree, [the wooden cross] *that we, being dead to sins, should live unto righteousness: by whose stripes ye were healed.*
I Peter 2:24

Rebekah's Birth

We still lived in the cold little town in Wyoming when Rebekah was born in 1980. I went to the same physician that had delivered Adam. There was one difference. A civic group had raised money to purchase a fetal heart monitor for our small hospital. Most people were pleased. Not me, I didn't like the thought of being tied down with wires.

I had asked the doctor several times if I could please be excused from using that machine. Every time his answer was the same, "No. I think it would be best for your baby."

Of course I wanted what was best for my baby. That's why I planned to not use any drugs during the delivery. I believed that Jesus had redeemed me from the curse of pain in childbirth (Genesis 3:16, Galatians 3:13). I believed that childbirth should be as natural as possible, and wires just weren't part of my natural.

So, I prayed, "Dear God, I do want what's best for my baby and I know You do too. I submit to your perfect will in this matter. If I don't have to use it, that would be great. If I need to use it, please help me get through it, in Jesus' holy name. Amen"

Rebekah arrived on her due date in April. Leigh and I took Adam to my best friend's home and then we drove to the hospital. An interesting thing about the hospital is that when it was being built, they didn't really plan for a large maternity unit. They'd simply put up a wall, down the middle of the hall to the operating room. It divided the short hall leaving half the space as a hall and the other half was the tiny little labor room.

When we arrived at the hospital, I was in pretty advanced labor. They put me on a gurney, prepped me, and left me in the hall right outside the only labor room, with profuse apologies. However, I was delighted!

It just so happened that the fetal heart monitor was being repaired that afternoon. The repairman had all the pieces and wires spread out all over the bed in the tiny labor room. I was so thankful. It didn't matter that I was lying in the hall. The words of Psalms 116:1 were washing over me, *I love the LORD, because He hath heard my voice and my supplication.*

When it was delivery time, the doctor was even willing to not clamp my feet into the stirrups if I'd leave them up there. I did. Rebekah Leigh Nelson was born without any complications or drugs being needed. Her body temperature was a little low, so they put her in an incubator.

I had made arrangements to have this baby room-in with me, but I couldn't have her until her temperature was warmer. As soon as I got to my hospital room, I called my praying friends and we all agreed in prayer for Rebekah's temperature to rise quickly and safely

God answered that prayer. In a few hours I was holding my precious little girl in my arms and she stayed in my hospital room with me.

It's always an interesting reminder to me of how God answered that prayer, because to this day, Rebekah's normal temperature is above 98.6 degrees. God is so good and I think He has quite a sense of humor.

Lo, children are an heritage from the LORD: and the fruit of the womb is His reward.
Psalms 127:3

God of Hope

$\mathscr{I}$ can remember the decisive moment very clearly. I had come home from the hospital with our beautiful baby daughter, Rebekah. My mom had gladly flown from Montana to help take care of Adam.

It was really important to me that Adam, 27 months old, didn't feel displaced by our new baby. So, when I found out I was pregnant, I began telling Adam, "Momma's going to have another baby and then we will have *two* babies to love in this family."

Now Adam was contentedly playing in his room with his Grandma Bev's rapt attention. Leigh was at work. I was lying on my bed, nursing Rebekah, and silently crying out to God about my broken heart.

It was not post-partum blues. I was delighted to be a mother of two.

Our marriage had always been a difficult challenging time for me. Leigh has given me permission to tell the truth in hopes that others can learn and avoid much heartache. When we were married, Leigh was very immature. Unfortunately, neither of us realized this and we enabled his spoiled selfish behavior to go pretty much unchecked.

At this time in our lives we were at an all-time low. He was in love with someone else. They weren't involved sexually, but she had his heart. I didn't even know what was going on then, but I knew something was terribly wrong and my heart was lonely, confused, and broken.

Later in our lives, Leigh told me that he would have left me for the other woman except that I was pregnant with Rebekah so he didn't think that would be the right time. This wasn't just a slight hiccup in our relationship. It was devastating. I felt so forsaken. Part of me just wanted to die, but I knew my children needed a good mom.

That's why I was crying out to God. I felt hopeless and I needed some very strong help. I knew it could only come from God and His Word quickened by His Holy Spirit, but I had no idea where to look. I desperately opened my Bible and the first verse that I saw was Romans 15:13, *Now the God of hope fill you with all joy and peace in believing, that ye may abound in hope, through the power of the Holy Spirit.*

In that desperate moment, I reasoned that if God was the God of hope, and I had just read that He was, then He must have enough hope for me right now. That was the decisive moment. I chose to cling to His promise and He came through. I continued to cling to God and His hope.

That they might set their hope in God, and not forget the works of God,
Psalms 78:7a

Fern Fronds

To celebrate the birth of our daughter, Rebekah, our dear friends, Craig and Suzanne, gave us a hanging fern. It was a fascinating plant that sent out new fronds to uncurl. Soon there would be a beautiful display of tiny new leaves in an evenly balanced pattern trailing down a main stem.

It delighted me to see a new stem start to grow. They would often grow to be over five feet long, with the tiny leaves gracing the length of the stem, in beautiful symmetry.

Unfortunately, if the fern became too dry, the tiny leaves would quickly dry up, turn brown, and fall off, leaving the main stem as a long scraggly string. Since they were still alive, I didn't want to cut off the stringy stems, but they sure didn't look very good.

Then one day I noticed a new thing. One of the older stringy stems started to grow new leaves again in the beautiful pattern. I was grateful, but it was still the new shoots that delighted me.

My attitude changed when one evening the Creator showed me the parable of the fern. He explained to me that each frond was like a person being born into the kingdom of heaven. It is marvelous when one is born again.

But then the Lord spoke words to my heart that I'll never forget. He told me how much He loves to see new growth appear on an old frond, because that happens whenever a Believer allows God's Holy Spirit to breathe new life and growth into them. That is always His desire.

From then on, I realized that we all can give God delight by becoming more like Jesus, by allowing His Holy Spirit to manifest more forgiveness, more love, and more of His life in us. No matter how old we are, or how dry we may feel, with God all things are possible—even new beautiful growth.

But grow in grace, and in knowledge of our Lord and Savior, Jesus Christ.
To Him be glory both now and forever. Amen.
II Peter 3:18

Peaceful Children

As a new Christian Believer in college, I took copious notes from speakers, sermons, and Bible studies. However, I never really seemed to make time to go back and study most of those notes. God gave me a mind that can learn things very quickly. It is also a mind that works better with the least amount of clutter. That's one reason my home is usually very tidy, I can think better.

After about a year of studying the Bible, I realized that if I listened closely, I could understand and remember most things. If I felt the information was really important, I jotted a note in my Bible where I would be sure to see it again. It was pretty easy for me to memorize Scripture by just reading and repeating the verse a few times. It took longer to remember the addresses, or where they're found in the Bible.

I rarely used sticky notes or index cards, they seemed to clutter up my space and distract my mind. But there was one huge exception. Shortly after our son, Adam, was born, God made Isaiah 54:13 "leap off" the page!

It says, *"And all thy children shall be taught of the LORD; and great shall be the peace of thy children* (Isaiah 54:13).

That was such a huge promise for something that was of utmost importance to me. I wanted my children to really know God, to love Him, and to be loved by Him. So, I wrote the words of Isaiah 54:13 on a large 5 x 7" index card and put it on my fridge, where it stayed for almost 20 years! It got rather tattered, but it wasn't clutter.

God kept that promise to me. I started reading the Bible out loud to Adam, 2, and to Rebekah, a newborn infant, during our afternoon rest times. The three of us spent hours snuggled together in a wooden rocking chair that Leigh had given to me. I often nursed Rebekah while we read.

After we made it through my King James Version once, it was the only Bible I had at the time, I decided to buy an easier to understand version. We got the Living Bible by Kenneth Taylor. Ours had a red cover, so we all called it the "Red Bible."

We began reading at night before bedtime, then Leigh could hear it too, when he was in town. We started with Genesis 1:1 and Matthew 1:1. We continued to read a chapter from both the Old and New Testaments almost every single night, for the next eighteen years, until Rebekah left for college.

By the time Adam and Rebekah were in grade school we had worn out the Red Bible, so we began reading from the King James Version again. Every year we would read through the Old Testament about once and the

New Testament a couple of times. We hid the Word in our hearts and we lived the Word in our lives, basking in God's goodness and love.

Adam and Rebekah acted out Bible stories when they were young. We memorized so many verses. Later, when taking vocabulary tests at school, they often found that KJV had expanded their vocabularies and helped them excel on the tests. They really knew what God's Word said.

Both Adam and Rebekah were delightful and peaceful children. Neither went through terrible twos nor were they rebellious during the teenage years. Rebekah was a strong willed child, but God showed me that if she was trained up in godliness, she would be able to use her inner strength to resist ungodly peer pressure later in her life.

Another way that God gave us great peace was by teaching me the importance of the powerful yet simple prayer, "Let there be peace." After all, God created the heavens and earth with a few "Let there be" words, so I knew it was a powerful form of prayer.

Any time squabbles or irritability started up, I'd calmly and firmly pray "Let there be peace," and there was peace. I knew according to James 4:7 that I was resisting unclean spirits and they had to flee!

Raising godly, happy, healthy children was the most important and wonderful job to me. By God's grace, strength, and wisdom, I was a very consistent, firm, fair, and loving disciplinarian. That gave my children the comfort and safety of knowing they could expect to be protected and loved and enjoy a nurturing life. They also knew they were expected to obey and they did. As Hebrews 12:11 describes, fair disciplining *yields the peaceable fruit of righteousness.*

It was really important to me to fill our home, and their lives, with joy and activities. We didn't watch very much TV. We played games. We made things. We cooked and baked together. We rented movies that had uplifting themes. We read books together out loud and they both became wonderful readers. We had company often. Praise music usually played from our stereo or the radio. I found every occasion to celebrate. We even made banana splits on National Ice Cream Day.

We invited God's Holy Spirit to come into our home and into our lives with all His love, joy, peace, patience, kindness, goodness, faith and self-control (Galatians 5:22). He came and blessed us abundantly.

I will pour my Spirit upon thy seed, and my blessing upon thine
offspring.
Isaiah 44:3b

Better for Boo Boos

The first time Adam had a little boo-boo, God's Holy Spirit convinced me that to just "kiss it to make it better" was *not* the best choice. That idea probably got started for a very minor bump or scrape since usually nothing more is needed than to divert the child's attention away from it. The body can take care of the very minor injury.

However God's Holy Spirit taught me that it would be a much better choice to teach my son, and later my daughter, to do something that really could make a helpful difference even if it was a more serious situation. So whenever anyone experienced any kind of bump, scrape or boo-boo, we would pray, "Let there be no pain or damage in Jesus' holy name."

That was our powerful prayer any time there was a possibility of pain or injury. We lived very healthy, pain-free lives. There were only a couple of very minor accidents over the years, but God always answered our prayer.

Years later, I realized again how profound that teaching was when I accidentally stubbed my toe really hard in our kitchen in Moses Lake, Washington. Adam was about 6 years old at the time. As soon as I let out my cry of pain, Adam flew across the kitchen. He dropped to his knees in front of me, put his hands on my foot and prayed, "Let there be no pain or damage, in Jesus' holy name."

Immediately my toe was fine and I was so overjoyed by Adam's faith and actions! Decades later those are still the first words out of my mouth after any kind of accident or injury.

Out of the mouth of babes and sucklings hast thou ordained strength because of thine enemies, that thou mightest still the enemy and the avenger.
Psalms 8:2

Bold Brother

While I was praying one day, the Lord showed me the parable of the big bold brother. In this picture parable, I saw a young child who was afraid to walk down the sidewalk to get home because there were about half a dozen mean, big bullies leering and making threats. The child was actually so paralyzed with fear, he couldn't move.

Then along came the child's big, bold, strong, and caring brother. He was buff! Tall framed with huge muscles and a fearless, bold, determined look on his face that defied the bullies. The big bold brother simply took the child's hand and they both walked straight down the sidewalk, without a word or incident from any of the bullies. In fact every one of the bullies either left or turned away when the two walked toward them.

I understood the meaning of this one. Of course, every Believer could be the child. The sidewalk is God's will. The bullies are demons and others who are hostile to us, the godly people. The strong, big, bold, caring brother is none other than Jesus Christ, the Victor!

The Message Bible describes God's view of this in Psalms 89:21-23, *And I'll keep my hand steadily on him, yes, I'll stick with him through thick and thin. No enemy will get the best of him, no scoundrel will do him in.*

Let's remember Who goes with us on this life journey and take courage. We really never are alone. Remember, Jesus' precious final words before He ascended into heaven, *"Lo, I am with you always, even unto the end of the age. Amen."* Let's walk by faith and not by sight.

Ye are of God, little children, and have overcome them: because greater is He that is in you, than he that is in the world.
I John 4:4

Good Gifts

*D*uring our early months of marriage, we had agreed to tithe and to remain debt free, based on what the Bible taught about money (Malachi 3:10, Romans 13:8). We established our "bare bones" budget in order to save as much as possible. Our goal was to be able to pay cash for everything including major purchases, such as a car, and even a debt-free dream house someday.

We were still on that "bare bones" budget when we lived a very small town in Wyoming. For a few weeks, the local radio station played black-out bingo with the listeners. We used bingo cards that we received from the local merchants each week. The grand prize was a $50 shopping spree at any of the participating merchants. One Friday I won the grand prize!

Perhaps $50 sounds so small today, but in the late 1970's to a young stay-at-home wife who was feeding her family of three on less than $50 per month, and avoiding *all* unnecessary purchases, it was a huge gift!

As soon as I had called the radio station to verify my win, I fell on my face on the floor in our shabby little rental home to praise and thank God for this great gift. I firmly believed that the gift was from Him, since James 1:17 says, *Every good gift and every perfect gift is from above, and cometh down from the Father of lights, with whom there is no variableness, neither shadow of turning.*

While I was lying face down on the floor, my generous Heavenly Father gave me a vision. It was as if I was suspended in space and wonderful things were zooming at me extremely fast, coming from all directions. There were expensive things like gorgeous fur coats, stacks of money, shiny expensive cars, houses, tropical settings, and beautiful jewelry. It actually took my breath away and was almost overwhelming.

In some way that I didn't even quite understand, I knew those things were actually coming right to me. I remember telling God then and there, on my face before Him, that I didn't want any of those things if they would separate me from Him. His presence would always be the greatest gift and treasure to me. I also asked Him not to *ever* let anything come between Him and me.

I can honestly say that after living on the "bare bones" budget for nine years, we were able to pay cash for everything, including a new truck, a new car, and a custom built dream home with an indoor hot tub on a one acre lot in Washington state. We praised God for every wonderful thing about our new debt-free home.

Then about 15 years later we sold that place. We moved closer to Leigh's office and bought ten acres in a great school district. We built a new debt-free dream home with an indoor swimming pool and an outside tennis court. We had even more reasons to praise and thank the Generous Giver.

Over the years the Lord has also given me many things that I saw in the long ago vision such as jewelry, furs, wonderful family vacations in beautiful tropical locations, new cars, a condo in Hawaii, and many other wonderful gifts. But no gift has ever come close to overshadowing Him, the greatest of all good gifts!

If ye then, being evil, know how to give good gifts unto your children,
how much more shall your Father, who is in heaven, give good things to
them that ask Him?
Matthew 7:11

Logos and *Rhema*

In the original Greek there are two different words in the New Testament that are translated into English as "word." The *logos* is defined in a Greek lexicon as the power of the mind that is manifested in speech; thought, and reasoning.

God's power of the mind words were inspirationally written by about 40 authors in the books and letters which we call the Bible. That's His *logos* to us, and it is a wonderful word.

We are instructed to study that logos in II Timothy 3:15-16, *And that from a child thou hast known the holy scriptures, which are able to make thee wise unto salvation through faith which is in Christ Jesus. All scripture is given by inspiration of God, and is profitable for doctrine, for reproof, for correction, for instruction in righteousness.*

That verse explains that God inspired the writers of the Bible so that you and I can learn what is correct (doctrine), what is wrong (reproof), what to do to make things right (correction), and how to live a God honoring, victorious life (righteousness). That's His intent—for all of His children to experience God's *logos* word. *Logos* is extremely important.

In addition to the *logos* form of word, there is also the Greek word *rhema,* which comes from the verb meaning "to speak or to make an utterance." *Rhema* denotes a word that is specifically spoken at a certain time and space. That is the holy, mysterious, living, or quickened word that God speaks directly into our spirits. We do hear, but not necessarily with our fleshly ears.

We are instructed in Romans 10:17: *So, then, faith cometh by hearing, and hearing by the word of God.* When God speaks with a *rhema,* we must hear it with our spiritual ears. Born again Believers can learn to desire, discover, and discern this glorious intimate *rhema* from our Heavenly Daddy by spending time with Him. We learn to recognize His voice like we do other voices, by hearing it often.

Many people are frightened about such a mystical thing. They rightly believe that the enemy of our souls, the great deceiver, can also give us a *rhema.* Unfortunately, they decide to reject all *rhemas.*

That would be as foolish as deciding not to use any paper money because some of the bills might be counterfeit. I John 4:1 gives us this wise advise: *Beloved, believe not every spirit, but try* [test] *the spirits whether they are of God; because many false prophets are gone out into the world.*

God often uses the very words in His *logos* to give us a *rhema.* When you have heard a *rhema* from God you know that you have heard from

Him! Then you can take the next step of faith and believe that He means what He says. That's faith!

We need both types of words, the *logos* and the *rhema*. Without the Spirit's *rhema*, we'd dry up, without His *logos*, we might blow up.

For the Word that God speaks is alive and full of power [making it active, operative, energizing, and effective]; it is sharper than any two-edged sword, penetrating to the dividing line of the breath of life (soul) and [the immortal] spirit.
Hebrews 4:12a, Amplified Bible

Self-Cleaning Oven Faith

As odd as it may sound there is a lesson about faith in a self-cleaning oven. At least that's what the Lord showed me. The self-cleaning oven operates best according to the manufacturer's instructions, so does faith.

First of all, you have to believe that the oven really does have the self-cleaning capacity or you won't even bother trying it. You also need to believe that God has the capacity to do what He says He will do, or you won't even bother to give God the chance be God in your behalf.

Next, you don't just stand in front of the oven thinking, "I really believe this oven can clean itself." Nor should you just stand in front of any circumstance thinking, "I really believe God can do something." In both situations, you go to the instruction manual's specific directions. If you don't follow the oven cleaning directions it doesn't work. If you don't follow God's directions, faith doesn't work either.

Faith comes by hearing the Creator's living word and acting on it. The Bible is literally filled with God's ideas about how to live life in all kinds of situations. Sometimes you will have a situation that isn't exactly covered in the Bible. It's perfectly OK to get your Bible and honestly pray something like, "Dear God, I don't know what to do and I need to know what You want me to do in this situation. Please quicken Your Word to me now, in Jesus name. Amen."

Listen to see if He prompts you to a certain passage. If not, just open up your Bible and start reading until He makes something alive to you.

Hopefully this won't be the only way you read your Bible, but it *is* one valid way in certain circumstances. If you are diligently seeking God's will for your life, you will be reading and studying the Bible to learn His ways and principles. But don't totally disregard this impromptu type of reading.

After God quickens, or makes it really alive to you from the Bible, then you have something to put your faith into. Applying your faith to those words is like flipping the lever on the self-cleaning oven. That's what gets the process started.

Many people are surprised that I can go to the Bible to ask God for instructions or directions and get it from His Holy Spirit quickening, or making me to know, because He makes His written Word so alive. I am surprised that all Believers don't do that. Hopefully this book will show you that God desires to communicate with us. His Word is alive, and God's Word works.

So, then, faith cometh by hearing, and hearing by the word of God.
Romans 10:17

Useful Guardrails

We hit the icy patch and began spinning and sliding uncontrollably on the steep mountain road that didn't have guardrails. Leigh was driving our car. Adam and Rebekah were in the backseat. It was one of the most terrifying moments of my life. I earnestly, began praying loudly in the Spirit. Praise God our car stopped just before sliding off the cliff into the river below.

Ever since that frightening winter incident in Wyoming, I have been thankful for guardrails, especially on mountain passes. On a recent drive over Lookout Pass, between Montana and Idaho, the Lord showed me another picture parable.

His Word is to our lives what the guardrails are to the highway. Both are there to show the correct path and to help keep us safe!

So many people act like God's instructions are given to us because He just wants to wreck our lives with dull boring rules. Nothing could be further from the truth. He gives instructions so that we *can* live life safely, peacefully, and joyfully to the fullest. We don't have to be confused about which way to go or to be tentatively wondering if we are going over the edge any minute.

Jesus sets the record straight in John 10:10, *The thief comes only to steal, and to kill, and to destroy; I am come that they might have life, and that they might have it more abundantly.*

In Hosea 4:6a God boldly proclaims, *"My people are destroyed for lack of knowledge."*

How long until we, His people, act like God means what He says? Let's understand who is trying to destroy our lives and Who really knows, beyond a shadow of a doubt, how we can experience abundant, fulfilling, meaningful life.

God's Word makes all the difference. We must take the time to learn what He says and apply it. We must seek diligently to follow the leading of His Holy Spirit and respond quickly. That's how the guardrails are built into our lives and remain there for our guidance and protection, so we can really experience a full wonderful life.

Thy word is a lamp unto my feet, and a light unto my path.
Psalms 119:105

Teaching Certificate

I earned my elementary education degree from Montana State University. Then Leigh and I moved to Wyoming where I did some substitute teaching. Since I never had the desire, or felt God's leading to become a full time teacher, I didn't get a teaching certificate.

Then in December of 1982, we moved to Moses Lake, Washington. It was such a mild winter that we begin building our first dream home in March of 1983. When I say build, I do mean build. Leigh and I bought the book, How to Build a Wood-Frame House, by L. O. Anderson and we dug the foundation, poured concrete, sawed, hammered, wired, sheet rocked, plumbed, and painted. We did everything except lay the carpet and install the garage doors. That we had professionals do.

We also had a wonderful neighbor, Hugh who was a professional contractor. He gave us great advice and helped us hours on end, just because he liked us and was rather amazed that we were building a house using a book as our guide. His wife, Linda, was so kind that she let us use their bathroom whenever we needed until we had one of our own.

It was such a labor intensive work of love. It was also a dream come true for us to build that home debt-free. Right in the middle of all that joy and work and focus on building a house, the Lord unmistakably told me, "Get your Washington teaching certificate."

I'm ashamed to say that I procrastinated with God about that for a short season. I really still had no desire to teach full time. In fact, I could hardly wait to be a homemaker in my own home, after renting for nine years.

But God did not relent. His message was clear and strong, "Get your Washington teaching certificate now."

Finally, in late April, I asked my neighbor who was a full time teacher in that school district about getting my teaching certificate. She explained that I needed to fill out forms at the school's district office, then I'd need to substitute teach for a bunch of days before getting the certificate.

She also warned me, "It's very hard to get called to sub in Moses Lake schools. There are already plenty of good subs and most teachers have their favorites that know the routine."

Now I understood why God had wanted me to get going. I prayed for His perfect will to be done in this situation. I went to the district office to get the information, filled out the forms, and added my name to the substitute pool. I praised God all the way home!

I realized why He had been so insistent on getting my certificate at that time. There was a time limit on how far back they would take my education credits. I was at the limit. If I had I waited until the next school year, it would have been too late and my degree wouldn't have been sufficient, I would have needed to take many more education credits before I could be allowed to be a substitute teacher in that district.

I needed God's favor because I also had to get a certain number of days of substitute teaching experience in that school district to get the certificate. The school year was almost over, I would need to teach all but about five days left of the remaining school year.

Praise the Lord! I did get called in to sub and they kept calling me. I subbed enough days to get my Washington Teaching Certificate and it was exceedingly useful over the years. I loved subbing and was able to bless many students in scores of classrooms. God's timing was wonderful.

I will instruct thee and teach thee in the way which thou shalt go: I will guide you with mine eye.
Psalms 32:8

A Long Awaited Promise

*C*indy and I were both substitute teachers in the same school district. When we met she had been attending church for years but didn't have a very vibrant relationship with God. As we became closer friends, I had the joy of watching God make Himself alive to her through Jesus Christ. Cindy became an on fire Christian and a full time teacher.

I loved being a substitute teacher in her building because we'd eat lunch together in her room and visit about whatever was on our hearts. One day she turned my world right side up when she said to me, "You are the strongest Christian that I know. You always have a verse to overcome the devil except where Leigh is concerned. That's about the only way the devil attacks you, through your husband, Leigh."

Zing! She had spoken the truth in love. That opened my eyes to the truth in Ephesians 6:12, *For we wrestle not against flesh and blood, but against principalities, against powers, against the rulers of the darkness of this world, against spiritual wickedness in high places.*

Understanding that dynamic helped me to stop blaming myself for Leigh's behavior. I stopped expecting Leigh to be different. I realized we were dealing with something much more sinister than some bad habits, carelessness, and broken promises.

However, for several months, I pretty much floundered. I knew the Word was filled with verses describing what a good Christian marriage should look like. There were commands for husbands and wives. I knew it was a very important area to God since marriage is supposed to represent His Son, Jesus, and His bride, the believing church. Our marriage was nowhere close to what it was supposed to be.

The biggest problem to me was that I was doing everything I knew to do to be a great wife. I'd also read the Bible cover to cover dozens of times, and I didn't know of a single promise that God had in His Word for a wife about her marriage. So I didn't have any verse to stand on, to believe in, to fight the enemy with, and to win! I kept earnestly asking God to show me His truth.

He did. We were visiting our friends, Craig and Suzanne, in Kansas. Craig gave us a small book of God's promises and I began reading it. The Holy Spirit cleared His throat after I read Psalms 138:8, *The LORD will perfect that which concerneth me: thy mercy, O LORD, endureth forever: forsake not the works of thine own hands.*

God's Holy Spirit asked me, "Doesn't your marriage concern you?"

"Oh, yes!" I replied.

He instructed me, "Then hang on to this verse as your promise about your marriage."

I did for years. When attacks would come from the enemy, through Leigh, I clung to that promise and I *knew* that God Almighty would perfect that which concerned me. I didn't know how or when, but I *knew* He would.

That was enough to hold on to and not be overcome by evil. God did keep His promise to me, but that is another story, or perhaps another book!

I wait for the LORD, my soul doth wait, and in His word do I hope.
Psalms 130:5

Trapped in a Bird Cage

During a difficult time in our marriage, my God showed me a vision that helped to set me free.

My husband, Leigh, was struggling with shame, depression, and guilt. His despair had robbed him of joy and hope about life in general and about our marriage in particular. It took a terrible toll on me when he was so despondent and didn't even want to resist the evil or turn to God.

I was reading about David and when I got to II Samuel 22:2, *And he said, The LORD is my rock, and my fortress, and my deliverer,* I knew that same God would be my Deliverer too. He had done it before and He would do it again.

He did it with a vision in my mind as I waited expectantly and quietly before Him. My Deliverer, revealed the picture of a gigantic, black metal bird cage with Leigh and me inside it. Leigh was sitting on the wire bench with his head in his hands in despair and defeat. I was also in the cage, prodding Leigh to get out; pleading with him; trying to get him to be happy; begging him; pushing him; scolding him; trying to carry him; and doing anything and everything I could to try to make him want to leave the cage and lead us both out.

Nothing I did was having any kind of a positive effect on Leigh. It was exhausting me and quenching the Holy Spirit within me.

Then the Lord revealed something wonderful. He showed me that the door to the bird cage was wide open! Jesus had already opened it and we were free to leave.

He also made me to know that I could not make another person leave the cage. We each choose our emotions, but I was free to leave the emotional cage. No one could make me remain in that destructive cage. Furthermore, by leaving the emotional cage of despair and false guilt, I could demonstrate what a life of joy and peace looked like. That would be much more compelling for Leigh to leave than anything else I could do or say.

I flew out of the emotional cage that day into peace, joy, and personal responsibility. Praise the Lord!

If the Son therefore, shall make you free, ye shall be free indeed.
John 8:36

Monopoly Money

One Sunday morning, as I was preparing for church, the Lord told me to share this example with congregation that day. He told me to take some Monopoly money, at least $100, and take the same amount of real cash.

When it was time to share with the congregation, God instructed me to hold up the Monopoly money and ask, "Would anyone be excited to get this? Of course not, since most people would think, 'It's useless, it won't do me any good because it isn't real.'"

Then I was instructed to hold up the real cash and again ask, "Would anyone be excited to get this?"

There was interest.

Then the Lord God instructed me to tell the congregation, "Those are the two ways that people treat God's word. Far too many treat the words of the Bible as if they were Monopoly money, just useless, not real, and won't do any good. Yet God's words are indeed real and powerful!"

There are great blessings for those of us who know, beyond a shadow of a doubt, that II Timothy 3:16 really means that all scripture is given by inspiration of God and is profitable for doctrine, learning what's right; for reproof, learning what's wrong; for correction, learning how to make things right; and for instruction in righteousness, learning how to keep things right.

God's Word is indeed powerful, and gets things done. His Word is exactly what it takes every time for every situation. I am excited that God's Word works!

These were more noble than those in Thessalonica, in that they received the word with all readiness of mind, and searched the scriptures daily, whether those things were so.
Acts 17:11

Picnic Baskets

*E*ach of our lives could be seen as a picnic basket filled with all of our hopes, dreams, desires, thoughts, words, smiles, intentions, and kind actions. Every time you have an encounter with someone it is an opportunity to share something from your picnic basket.

We could be giving God great pleasure by sharing good things from our basket with others. How delightful to get to enjoy wonderful things from other people's baskets throughout our lives.

One problem is that some people don't want to ever open up their picnic basket to share anything with anyone else. Oh, they will happily come to the picnic of life and partake of whatever another is willing to prepare and share with them. They just simply have no desire to give anyone anything from their basket.

Such selfishness grieves God. Sooner or later emotional takers will disappoint and over burden others. Eventually the greedy person with the closed basket will end up lonely, feeling like there was supposed to be more to this picnic called life.

Another problem is that some people have never learned to receive good things from others. Fear, shame, or false duty makes them think that they must always be the givers. They will end up sad and exhausted. God wants us to learn to love and to be loved.

I prayed, wanting my children to learn to give and receive. God answered my prayers with the idea of King and Queen Days!

Every month on the date of our birthday, we got to be King or Queen, which meant we got excused from our daily chores. Others stepped in and did them for us. Favorite foods were prepared and we'd all try to do the things that the King or Queen desired. Everyone in the family got a royal day, every month. It was wonderful. We all learned to be better givers and receivers.

I'd like to encourage you to not let fear, greed, pride, or selfishness keep you from opening your picnic basket. Go to God and let Him help you pack your basket with wonderful things. Then get ready to participate in the picnic called life and open up your basket to bless others and to be blessed.

A man that hath friends must show himself friendly.
Proverbs 18:24a

Rebekah's Suspenders

*R*ebekah, my daughter, has always enjoyed shoes and clothes. When she could barely walk, she would slip into my wooden Dr. Scholl sandals and clomp around, wearing only her diapers, my shoes, and a grin from ear to ear. Even as a toddler she loved to change her clothes throughout the day.

As she grew up, we'd shop together for her clothes. Rebekah has always had wonderful artistic taste and a flair for fashion, even on a budget. One outfit gave us a very tangible lesson in wisdom and choices. It was a cute purple and grey plaid skirt with suspenders that went over a white scooped-neck top. She really wanted to wear that outfit for her third grade class photo.

I tried to explain that although it was a darling outfit in person, in the photo, which only showed her face and shoulders, it might not be very becoming. She had her heart set on wearing that outfit.

The Lord said, "Let her wear it, good will come of this."

She joyfully wore it to school for picture day. When the photos arrived, it was such a disappointment for her. Sure enough, the head shot only showed the top of the suspenders over a shirt that looked like an undershirt. It was not nearly as cute as she had hoped.

After that incident, whenever she was about to make a rather poor choice, but not a dangerous one, I'd say, "Well, Honey, I think this is like the suspenders' picture. You can do it if you want to, but I don't think it would be your best choice."

Praise the Lord! She would really think about her decision and almost always chose a better way than her original choice. She also learned that choices have consequences, some that aren't easily seen, until it is too late to change.

Today, decades later, Rebekah is still a delight to behold with her fashion statements. But even more importantly, she is a woman who almost always makes wise decisions that glorify God!

Point your kids in the right direction—when they're old they won't be lost.
Proverbs 22:6, The Message Bible

Mean or Good Guard

For Christmas 1988, we took our son, Adam, 10, our daughter, Rebekah, 8, and our nephew, Judd, 6, to Orlando, Florida to go to Disney World. We flew out of Spokane, Washington at 6:40 a.m. and reached Orlando that evening.

All three children had been wonderful travelers for over 14 hours at airports or in airplanes. By the time we had rented a car and arrived at our hotel at Lake Buena Vista, it was dark.

The hotel grounds looked beautiful with rolling hills, small ponds, and plants everywhere. As we were walking along the winding path to our room, the weary little travelers decided it would be great fun to roll down the grassy bank.

They looked like three little logs rolling and laughing. I stood watching them and laughing at their enjoyment, until a hotel guard swiftly approached me.

"Ma'am, those children must *not* roll on the grass," he informed me.

I quickly called all three children and explained, "It's against the rules to be rolling on the grass, so let's think of something else fun to do inside the hotel."

I was silently thinking, "Boy, what kind of stuffy place is this with such a mean guard?"

The next morning on our way to breakfast, we were meandering along the same winding paths at the hotel. Suddenly I stopped and pointed to a small sign not far from where the children had been rolling last night.

The sign clearly stated:

> Do not swim.
> Do not wade.
> Do not feed the alligators.

Wow! I realized in an instant that the guard last night had *not* been being stuffy or mean. He had been a good guard protecting my children from being attacked by alligators who were known to be on the premises. We had been clueless. I later learned that the alligators moved about, especially at night, from one pond to another. I spent the rest of our vacation on very diligent "alligator patrol."

Too often we can think, when God tells us *not* to do something, that He is also being stuffy or mean. No He isn't. Someday we will see God and we will know as we are known (I Corinthians 13:12). We'll understand so much more than we do now. We will clearly see that God, in His infinite wisdom, love, and knowledge, said, "No," to protect us from harm.

Let's learn quickly that God is good. God is very wise. His decisions are right on target. God's Word works!

Therefore I esteem all thy precepts concerning all things to be right; and I hate every false way. The testimonies that thou hast commanded are righteous and very faithful.
Psalms 119:128 & 138

It's OK to Ask Why

There's a crippling idea being taught. Many teach that it is wrong to ask God "Why?"

I strongly disagree with that. I believe that we should approach God with utmost respect and honor. We certainly are not to be rude, demanding, or insolent when we talk to our Heavenly Father. However, we do get to be totally honest with Him.

After all, He already knows what we're thinking and feeling. So when something has happened, that we don't understand, it is honest and OK to ask God, "Why?"

Most people who teach that it is wrong to ask "Why?" imply that the question shows a lack of faith in God's sovereignty, or supreme authority. I sometimes wonder if the people teaching that wrong idea are afraid that God won't answer such a question.

I totally disagree. God is *not* afraid of that question or any question that we could ask, especially when we ask questions to better understand what His will is, so that we can be wiser, more obedient children.

God, in His supreme brilliance has given us His Word to help us understand Him and His ways. We need to believe that He does have an answer and that He is willing to tell us. There are several verses that confirm this to me:

Psalms 91:15: *He shall call upon me, and I will answer him: I will be with him in trouble; I will deliver him, and honor him.*

Psalms 99:8a: *Thou answeredst them, O LORD our God:*

Romans 11:4a: *But what saith the answer of God unto him?*

James 1:5-7:*If any of you lack wisdom, let him ask of God, who giveth to all liberally, and upbraideth not; and it shall be given him. But let him ask in faith, nothing wavering. For he that wavereth is like a wave of the sea driven with the wind and tossed. For let not that man think that he shall receive anything of the Lord.*

Those verses in James, clearly show that if you don't know what or why, then ask God. However, it's important to ask Him believing that He will answer you. He wants to answer you. He wants you to know His wisdom.

In fact, God has strongly warned us, in Hosea 4:6a, *My people are destroyed for lack of knowledge; because thou hast rejected knowledge, I will also reject thee.*

That's strong!

When we ask for God's wisdom, we are asking for something very special. Are you willing to pay a price? Are you willing to read the Bible searching for the truth? Are you willing to fast and pray until you find the answer? That's how I go after the truth, and He answers me.

One final thought on questions to God. Perhaps if we asked "What shall I do?" more often, then waited to obey His answer, we would need to ask "Why?" much less often.

Hear, O LORD, when I cry with my voice; have mercy also upon me, and answer me.
Psalms 27:7

A Calf Named Mercy

"*R*emember, Leigh, we're just *looking* at the calves for sale today," I reminded my husband as we drove to the nearby livestock auction on sale day. We already had eight cows on our eight acres of pasture, so we didn't really need another cow. That didn't seem to matter when the darling little buff-colored calf entered the sales pen.

We were sitting in the front row when she trotted over to us and looked up with huge soft eyes. We knew then that we would buy that calf, and we did.

"Sold!" the auctioneer cried.

Our excitement soon turned to dismay, as we realized that we had come to the sale in our Camaro sports car. How would we get our new calf home?

Then a friend, Jess Seibert, came over to congratulate us on the fine young heifer. It just so happened, that Jess had driven to the sale in a truck with a trailer and he hadn't bought anything. Since he would go right by our place on his way home, Jess readily agreed to deliver the calf.

When he reached our place, we signaled Jess to back up to the pasture gate and then we opened both our gate and his trailer. Out bounded the newest addition to our herd. She continued to race across the entire pasture, through the electric fence, across the highway with cars zipping by at 60 plus miles per hour, and into the corn field across the highway.

Our family, along with the neighbors, spent the next several hot hours searching for our little tan colored calf among the sixty acres of tan colored cornstalks towering over eight feet tall. Whenever we did sight her, she would get startled and run down another row. As the sun was setting, we finally realized that it would be almost impossible to find the new calf and bring her back. Sadly, we returned home.

Leigh groaned, "We were so foolish not confining the new calf to a pen for her first few days, so she could get used to her new home."

That evening as I was praying before going to sleep, I asked God to please protect the young calf and to let His perfect will be done.

As soon as I had prayed, God showed me a vision of an angel who stood calmly facing our calf in the cornfield. The angel, who looked like a young man with golden tanned skin, walked right up to the calf and lifted her up in both of his strong arms. Then he turned, flew across the highway while carrying the calf, and brought her back to our place.

After seeing that vision, I felt such a deep sense of God's all powerful presence. I turned to Leigh, who figured we would never see the calf again, and softly whispered, "With God all things are possible."

Then I slept peacefully. At 3 a.m., I was awakened by a mooing sound. I woke Leigh up, he heard it too. We both raced to look out the door. There was our beautiful little calf, calmly standing in our pasture, mooing!

Later that morning, when Adam and Rebekah woke up, we were rejoicing and deciding what to name our new calf. We realized that it had been God's great mercy that had brought her back to our place, so, we all agreed that her name should be Mercy.

That was three summers ago, and as I sit here writing, Mercy is in the pasture, just outside my window, calmly nursing her newest baby calf, Grace.

And Jesus, looking upon them, saith, With men it is impossible, but not with God; for with God all things are possible.
Mark 10:27

Shore Reflections

I was a beautiful sunny day in the Columbia Basin of Washington state. My family was enjoying the summer in our boat on Long Lake. As I sat relaxing in the boat, looking at the scenic shore with the towering cliffs and various trees and shrubs, the Lord taught me something interesting.

I noticed that the reflections in the water were all over the lake on such a beautiful, calm, sunny day. The reflections nearest the shore were the clearest. They almost looked like a mirror image of the shore line. As the reflection stretched out further into the lake, the image was still of the shore but it became blurrier the further out I looked.

Then the Lord made me to know that it was much like being close to Him. Those people who spend much time with Jesus and are very close to Him, will reflect a clear picture of what Jesus Christ is really like. They are the people who spend time reading and obeying His Word, letting His truth transform their mind and actions (Romans 12:2).

They are in close communication with Him. They will have His characteristics such as love, joy, peace, patience, gentleness, goodness, faith, meekness, and self-control (Galatians 5:22-23). They will have that same desire to please our Heavenly Father. They will know the will of God for their lives and do it (John 4:34).

The Believers who spend *some* time with Jesus will still reflect His image, but it won't be as clear, especially when trials and temptations arise. The further people are from Jesus, the blurrier the reflection becomes.

Seeing such a vivid picture of reflections really encouraged me to want to be as close to Jesus as I can be. I really want other people to see more clearly just how outstanding Jesus Christ really is!

Be ye, therefore, followers [literally, imitators] *of God, as dear children; and walk in love, as Christ also hath loved us, and hath given himself for us an offering and a sacrifice to God for a sweet-smelling savor.*
Ephesians 5:1-2

Shield of Faith

*W*hile I was praying for the needs of a member in our Bible study, the Lord showed me a parable of Ephesians 6:16, *Above all, taking the shield of faith, with which ye shall be able to quench all the fiery darts of the wicked.*

I had claimed that verse for myself many times and I was always thankful that it said that we could quench *all* the fiery darts, not just some of them. This time God showed me how I can help protect another person.

In the parable picture that God showed me, the fiery darts aimed at my friend were stopped and became harmless when they reached what I was holding—a strong shield of faith in God and faith in His Word. As I was using my faith in God's goodness, power, and provision to pray for my fellow Believer whose faith in that area wasn't as strong yet, it was as if I was stepping in front of that person and the deflecting the evil darts.

I knew beyond a shadow of a doubt that our God would provide and protect my friend and that the evil could not prevail. As it turned out, that is exactly what happened.

The Lord showed me that at times when our individual faith isn't strong enough to resist the evil, other Believers can shield each other. Then when even the faith of others is not enough, Jesus Christ, our High Priest, is praying for us.

That's what Hebrews 7:25 assures us, *Wherefore, He* [Jesus] *is able also to save them to the uttermost that come unto God by Him, seeing He ever lives to make intercession for them.*

I can assure you that when Jesus steps between evil and us, His shield of faith is definitely strong enough to quench *all* the fiery darts of the wicked. Isn't it magnificent that Jesus is in heaven praying for you and me right now?

Confess your faults one to another, and pray one for another, that ye may be healed. The effectual fervent prayer of a righteous man availeth [accomplishes] *much.*
James 5:16

Savor the Word

"*The* average Christian in America owns three Bibles, but rarely reads any of them," the radio DJ cited from a recent survey.

I thought, "Then it's no wonder that God doesn't seem very real or close to most people."

Unfortunately many people are totally unaware of what a powerful force the Bible can be in their lives. *You shall know the truth and the truth shall make you free,* isn't a cute saying, it is the absolute truth (John 8:32).

However, the knowing must come before the freedom comes. It is imperative for Believers to spend time reading the Bible, and especially reading it in ways that please God. I discovered one of those ways and it has helped make the Bible very powerful in my life.

I read the famous encounter in Matthew 16:23 where Jesus replied to Peter, *"Get thee behind me, Satan."* I had read that many times before, but, as it should be when one is reading a living word, something came alive. That day the words that followed Jesus' famous rebuke are what stood out to me. Do you know what else Jesus said in that very same verse? It could make a huge difference in the way you read the Bible.

Jesus goes on to tell Peter that he is an *offense* to Him because Peter *does not savor the things of God,* instead of the things of men. Wow! In all the years of hearing sermons on that encounter, and reading it for myself, I had never before seen those strong words showing how disgusted God is when we do not savor His things.

I pondered what it meant to savor a delicious food. Think of your favorite food right now. Is your mouth watering with pleasure and anticipation? Is that how you treat the Word of God? I hope so. Savoring also implies a special penchant to see things from God's perspective instead of how man sees things. Do you realize that it is an offense to God to *not* view things that way?

I hadn't been savoring things of God but I did *not* want to be an offense to Him. So, I prayed, "Dear Lord, please forgive me for not savoring the things of You enough. Please help me to savor Your things much more than I do the things of men, in Jesus' name. Amen."

I continued reading, fully expecting to savor more in the future. I had no idea how soon the future would be. Exactly one chapter later, in Matthew 17:23, God let me savor something! He also showed me what a huge emotional difference savoring His things will make to us.

In Mt. 17:22, Jesus explains to His disciples what is going to happen to Him—He will be betrayed, killed, and then be raised from the dead. After hearing that, we are told in the next verse, the disciples were very depressed. By not savoring the things of God, but rather viewing from man's perspective, they became really depressed and grieved God.

If they had savored the things of God, they would have been intrigued not depressed. They probably would have peppered Jesus with questions like, "Does that mean that even after they've killed you, you will really be alive again?" "How will you do that?" "What will you be doing during those three days?"

They would have been filled with wonder, excitement, and courageous anticipation. They would have been pleasing God, not offending Him.

Since then I have tried to remember to pray that God will make me to savor His things every time I read the Bible. It does make a wonderful difference. I believe that if you ask God to help you savor His Word, He will.

Then opened He their understanding, that they might understand the scriptures.
Luke 24:45

Easter Revelation

While living in Moses Lake, Washington, I once attended the city-wide sunrise Easter service at the county fairgrounds. The rest of my family opted not to go to that early service. So, I was sitting quietly amongst strangers on the bleachers in the grandstand while I was beholding the beauty of the early morning. I was silently praising God for making it so gorgeous for us.

Before the service began, the Lord asked me, "Do you know what My favorite thing in all of creation is?"

I sat there looking at the glorious sky, and wondered if maybe it was the sky with the incredible sun and planets and moon.

"No," He said.

I thought of mighty oceans and considered those.

"No," again.

I could see many trees across the town and gave that a thought, but somehow I knew that wasn't it. I also wondered about gorgeous flowers. And then the thought of all the animals was intriguing.

However, I realized that I didn't really have any idea what would be the Creator's favorite. So, I honestly answered, "No, I don't know. What is Your favorite creation, in Jesus' name?"

Quickly and with such a loving voice He answered, "People."

I thought "Oh, I should have known that! After all, we're created in His image and He became one of us. And what a sacrifice He made so that we could become His children."

That simple little guessing game on such a splendid day has always stuck with me. It reminds me of just how precious people are to God

Sometimes people can be so difficult and act so unlovely. Those are the times I remember that hurting people often hurt others. Then I just remember how much He loves them. It helps me to be a little more patient with them and appreciate them more. I know how really important they are to Him.

When I consider the heavens, the work of thy fingers, the moon and the stars, which thou hast ordained. What is man, that thou are mindful of him? And the son of man, that thou visitest him, ... and hast crowned him with glory and honour.
Psalms 8:3-5b

Healed Hand

The bee stung my finger just below my wedding band. I prayed for healing and forgot about it, since we were getting ready for a trip. That night in the hotel, I noticed that my stung finger was getting very swollen. It was also turning numb. I couldn't even move my rings. I was concerned that circulation was being cut off. I was wondering if I might have to have my wedding rings cut off to save my finger.

I didn't know any doctors, or jewelers, in that city. But I knew God and I knew that He would have a good plan for me so I grabbed my Bible and asked, "What do I do, Dear God, in Jesus name?"

I flipped opened my Bible. The first verse I saw was Matthew 12:13, *Then saith* [Jesus] *to the man, Stretch forth thine hand. And he stretched it forth; and it was restored whole, like the other.*

I *knew* God was going to heal my hand. So, I stretched forth my hand to the ceiling, figuring that was the direction to His heavenly throne, and I read that verse out loud. Praise God, most of the swelling immediately went down and the numbness turned to tingling. However, the wedding rings were still a little too tight. I could just barely move them around.

Now here's the rest of the story, when I was reading that verse, Matthew 12:13, I definitely heard God's Holy Spirit say, "Stop," after the word "*whole,*" but my eyes just kept going and I finished reading out loud the verse's last three words, "*like the other.*"

Then God had to correct me. He showed me how imperative it is that I stop when He says stop, even if I'm reading the Bible. You see, my left hand has always been a size smaller than my right hand. So God wasn't planning on restoring it '*like the other*', which was still too big. He wanted me to stop at, "*it was restored whole*" then He would make it the right size.

I realized that I had disobeyed God, while He was trying to heal me! I confessed my sin of disobedience and asked for His forgiveness. Then I reached out my left hand toward heaven and read Matthew 12:13 stopping where I was supposed to stop, "*Then saith* [Jesus] *to the man, Stretch forth thine hand. And he stretched it forth; and it was restored whole.*"

Praise the Lord! Obeying Him brought complete healing. My finger became its normal size, the tingling was gone, and I could turn my rings easily around that finger. Not only was my hand healed, I'd learned a very important lesson about carefully listening to God's instructions.

He sent His word, and healed them, and delivered them from their destructions.
Psalms 107:20

Home Run Apology

God taught me the parable of a home run apology and it has helped many find healing and wholeness through forgiveness. There had been a long season in our lives when my husband, Leigh, would say or do very hurtful things to me. I'd confront him about it, and he'd say, "I'm sorry. Please forgive me."

Unfortunately, his apology seemed to say "I'm sorry I was caught. Let's get this over with, quickly."

I knew God wanted me to forgive "seventy times seven" (Matthew 18:21-22). So, I would forgive Leigh again, and again, and again. Yet a hurt and frustration was building inside me. So, I prayed and asked God what we needed to do.

His answer surprised me, "You need to learn about Home Run Apologies."

I asked, "What on earth are those, Dear Lord, in Jesus' name?"

Then He showed me that when Leigh had hurt me, for Leigh to quickly say "I'm sorry, please forgive me," was like a baseball batter hitting the ball, running to *third* base, and back to home plate. It doesn't count for much in baseball, or in apologies.

The Lord showed me a much better way, using a baseball diamond as the parable. To get to first base, the one seeking forgiveness must admit "I was wrong to. . ." or "It was wrong of me to. . ."

Next, to get to second base, one must acknowledge how the behavior affected the offended person. For example "I understand that you feel really grieved, hurt, ignored, etc."

Then it's time to head to third base by saying "I'm sorry."

To complete the home run ask, "Will you please forgive me?"

When done sincerely, this apology will get a person back to home plate with the kind of an apology that really scores in true forgiveness and healing. We actually put a picture of a baseball diagram, with the appropriate statements at each base, on the refrigerator as a reminder for all of us to use with each other, and with God, when we needed to ask for forgiveness.

If someone forgot and reverted to the unhelpful, sneaky third base type of apology, we'd simply say "I need a home run apology."

Take heed to yourselves: If thy brother trespass against thee, rebuke him;
and if he repent, forgive him.
Luke 17:3

Home Run Apology Diamond

The idea of a Home Run Apology was so helpful to my family and the friends that we shared it with, that I talked to the editor of a Christian family magazine at a writer's conference. I gave her permission to print it in letters to the editor if she wanted to. I don't know if it was printed. Here's a diagram you might want to enlarge and use when necessary.

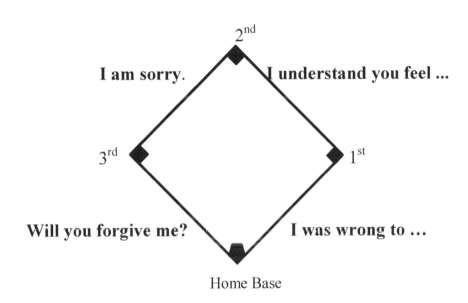

If ye know these things, happy are ye if ye do them.
John 13:17

Christian Husbands, Beware

*D*o you remember what the Bible tells us about Moses? He had a life filled with remarkable experiences with God Almighty. Exodus 33:11 tells us that the LORD spoke to Moses face to face, as a man speaks to his friend. Later, we learn in Exodus 33:17-23, that Moses asked to see God's glory and God said that He would do that for Moses because Moses had found grace in God's sight and God knew him by name. Moses was the one who spent forty seven days up on Mt. Sinai getting the Ten Commandments

Suffice it to say, Moses had a very real, personal, close relationship with God. Yet, even after walking close to God for 80 years, he did *not* get to enter into the Promised Land (Deut. 34:4). Why was that? It was because Moses disobeyed God about a very specific thing near and dear to God's heart—a type, or example, of Jesus Christ.

In Exodus 17:6, Moses obeyed God and struck the rock once to let the water come gushing out into the arid wilderness. Then, in Numbers 20:1-13, the Israelites were in a new part of the desert without water. They were grumbling and furious with Moses. So, Moses and Aaron fell on their faces before God. Then God instructed Moses to take the rod, and *speak* to the rock so it would give forth water (Numbers 20:8).

But, as we learn in Psalms 106:32-33, Moses was so provoked at the people that he said the wrong thing and struck the rock twice. The water came, but so did God's wrath at Moses and Aaron (Numbers 20:12). They were told that they would *not* get to go into the Promised Land. They didn't enter in. They both died before the Israelites went into the Promised Land.

You might wonder why hitting a rock twice was such a big deal to God. Well, the rock symbolized Jesus Christ who was to be crucified once. After that we go to Him and ask for our needs to be met. God was furious that the type of His Son was not displayed correctly before the people.

Now let's look at the instructions for godly living described in Ephesians 5:18-33. Please note especially verse 25, *Husbands, love your wives, even as Christ also loved the church, and gave Himself for it.*

In verse 32, the mystery is explained and revealed. God is using Christian marriages to be the best example that the world will ever see regarding what Jesus Christ is like towards His church. Undoubtedly, God is setting up Christian husbands to be the very example of His Son Jesus, as they relate to their wives in the ways God desires. It's much easier to see the correlation in this example than in the hitting/speaking to a rock example.

Do you think God takes the loving, protective, self-sacrificing husband type any less seriously than He did the rock type? Absolutely not!

Romans 15:4a, clearly explains *for whatsoever things were written aforetime* [in the Old Testament] w*ere written for our learning.* Let's pray that husbands can learn from Moses' mistake.

The Amplified Bible makes it very clear in I Peter 3:7, that God won't even honor the prayers of a mean, inconsiderate, selfish husband. *In the same way you married men should live considerately with [your wives], with an intelligent recognition of the [marriage relationship], honoring the woman as [physically] the weaker, but [realizing that you] are joint heirs of the grace (God's unmerited favor) of life, in order that your prayers may not be hindered and cut off. [Otherwise you cannot pray effectively.]*

In the documentary film, "The Lazarus Phenomenon," pastor Daniel Ekechukwu tells us his true story. During an argument with his wife, she slapped him. He was furious at her. The next day, when she was sorry and apologized, he remained furious and unforgiving. Then he left to take care of pastoral projects. He had a fatal car accident. Pastor Daniel was dead and embalmed. Three days later Daniel Ekechukwu was brought back to life!

During his death experience, he got revelation that because of his unforgiving, hard-hearted actions towards his wife, if he had remained dead, he would *not* have been allowed into heaven. It was his wife's faith that arranged for him to be brought back to life. He is a much kinder, gentler husband nowadays.

It is high time that Believers in Jesus Christ begin to hold husbands responsible for their physical, emotional, verbal, and sexual abuse of their wives. Such cruel, selfish, ungodly behavior is *not* acceptable to God and He takes it very seriously.

Be ye, therefore, followers of God, as dear children; and walk in love, as Christ also hath loved us, and hath given Himself for us an offering and a sacrifice to God for a sweet-smelling savor.
Ephesians 5:1-2

Crossed or Outstretched

*L*eigh and I had experienced another round of hurt between us. The details aren't so important but what God showed me about how to minimize the time lost to the enemy is important.

One of the destructive patterns that we would get into looked something like this. Even after a great deal of teaching about true godly living as a husband and wife, Leigh would often slip into treating me with neglect and contempt. I would become hurt and angry. Then he'd become hurt, angry, withdrawn, and silent.

I had learned the importance of speaking the truth in love, and I did my best to accomplish that. Speaking truth was easy. Speaking it in love was the challenge.

Leigh would listen, agree with me that he'd sinned against me, and then it was as if he went into zombie mode. He's explained that in those times, he's mad at himself, ashamed, discouraged, and then gets furious at me.

To me, it seemed perfectly obvious what had happened and what was necessary to change it. I figured it was obvious to Leigh too. It seemed that since he had done the wrong, it was up to him to make restitution. I was becoming impatient and disgusted that it was taking him so long to do the right thing!

Then God showed me a picture that changed the way I would react to Leigh, especially after there had been hurt between us. In the picture, Leigh and I were climbing a very steep rocky mountain. The destructive pattern played out again as we were climbing up to a common goal.

Afterwards, I stood there with my arms folded across my chest, tapping my foot, waiting for Leigh to do right and be my heroic godly leader. I wanted him to scale the distance between us and, in one graceful leap, get us out of the mess and back onto the trail of godly living.

I don't know that I took that posture physically, but I certainly had done it mentally! Then God showed me a better way.

Instead of just standing there, waiting for Leigh to figure it out, act on truth, and do something, all while I'm impatiently tapping my foot with my arms crossed. I saw myself gently reach out to him and offer my hand with a smile, and offer words of hope. Then he was able to accept the help and resume the hike up the hill into God's perfect will, instead of being paralyzed by shame, guilt, fear, or anger.

If I wait with my arms crossed, it may take others a long time to want to live a godly life, even if it would be the right thing for them to do. If I recognize that the enemy is trying to kill, steal, and destroy the good (John

10:10), I can quickly and gently do my part to stop the destruction and make things more loving, godly, and more conducive for others to choose the godly way.

Brethren, if a man be overtaken in a fault, ye who are spiritual, restore such an one in the spirit of meekness; considering thyself, lest thou also be tempted.
Galatians 6:1

$99 College Car

August, 1998, Adam, our son, was heading back to college in five days. Instead of returning to Rose Hulman Institute of Technology across the nation, where plane tickets had been the best kind of transportation, he would be transferring to Montana State University in Bozeman. That meant that a car would be great for him. Not only could he drive to college from home, but he could also drive two or three hours from college to visit both grandmas who also lived in Montana.

Adam and his dad had been rebuilding an Austin Healy car that Adam had bought literally in cardboard boxes years ago. They had done a great job of restoring it, but due to a serious clutch problem, it was now sadly obvious that the little car would *not* be ready in five days. Besides it was a small convertible and how could that haul everything to his dorm and keep him warm driving in the cold Montana winters?

Since we were paying for everything, including college, on a debt-free basis, there was only about $2000 extra dollars to buy a car. So I did what I've learned to do when there is a situation that needs a solution—I asked God to show me His perfect will in His Word about the situation. I was expectantly reading my Bible early that Friday morning, when, suddenly the words from Proverbs 8:20-21 leaped out at me, *I lead in the way of righteousness, in the midst of the paths of justice, That I may cause those who love me to inherit substance; and I will fill their treasuries.*

Looking around at all the beautiful things in my living room that really were treasures to me, I knew God already had filled my treasury many, many times. So with grateful faith I simply prayed to God, "You have indeed given me so much substance and treasure! Thank you! Now I just need You to fill the garage with a car that Adam can drive to college. And I only have $2000 extra dollars to buy it. Thank You for what You will do, in Jesus' name. Amen."

I was so excited that I could hardly wait for my family to wake up! I told them about the verse God had shown me and suggested that we go buy a car that very day. That afternoon we drove to Ephrata, where we saw a used station wagon for $2000. It was so dilapidated that we didn't even get out of our car to look at it.

We drove to nearby Moses Lake to take our daughter, Rebekah, to her waitress job. Then we could check out cars, before attending opening night at the Grant County Fair. On the drive Adam and Rebekah were looking through the newspaper when they found an ad for a dealership that would sell a car for $99 at 5 p.m. that day. We were so excited.

Rebekah's shift at the restaurant began earlier, so after dropping her off, the three of us headed to the dealership. There we learned that one car had already been chosen to be sold for only $99 to the person sitting in it at 5 p.m. Each person could choose any car and then they'd announce which car it was.

The salesmen told us they'd had a similar sale in January and the place had been packed with people. But this time, since it was opening day at the fair, there were only six customers and three of them were Nelsons!

"What great odds!" I thought. We all scurried to the used car that we hoped would be the $99 special among the hundreds of cars on the lot. Each of us got into a different used car just before 5 p.m.

Towards the back of the lot, I had selected a yellow car since that was Adam's favorite color. From my view point, I couldn't see where anyone else went. I was checking my watch, it was almost 5 p.m. All of a sudden, the Lord spoke clearly to me, "Pray in the Spirit."

So I began praying earnestly in the Spirit for about six or seven minutes, until He said, "That's enough."

I got out of the car, found Leigh, and we walked towards the front of the lot. Then I learned the rest of the story that had occurred while I was following God's instructions to pray.

It turned out that none of us had chosen the $99 car—a 1989 maroon Pontiac Grand Am. So, the manager pointed it out, several rows away from the front door and invited everyone interested to have a foot race from the front sidewalk. Leigh and I had been so far in the back of the lot that we weren't involved. The lady declined.

That left three for the race. Adam who was built like a linebacker, a tall young man who looked like a track star, and another shorter older man would be the racers.

The race began. The three men took off running. After a few steps the older man started coughing and stopped to light a cigarette,. A short time later, the long legged "track star" broke his sandal and quit running. Adam kept running and won the right to buy the $99 car! We did buy it and it was in great shape.

It only needed a new oil gasket and a lock for the trunk. We decided to also buy new tires. I still had most of my $2000 left over. Adam drove that car for five more years with minimal upkeep. I have continued to praise the One who fills my treasuries and at times, even my garage.

But my God shall supply all your need according to His riches in glory by Christ Jesus.
Philippians 4:19

Dripping Icicle

It was well below freezing outside and there were several glistening icicles of various lengths hanging from the eaves of our home. I couldn't believe my eyes. One and only one icicle was dripping. The Lord's Spirit spoke to me as I watched in awe, at the steady dripping of that unique icicle.

He told me to notice the cold freezing conditions that surrounded that icicle. Other icicles not far from that one were not dripping at all. They were frozen solid, cold and hard, like some people's hearts.

I wondered, "What makes that one icicle so warm that it's happily dripping regardless of the low temperature?"

Then I saw the truth He was trying to teach me. It was encouraging.

That icicle was in the full exposure of the sun's rays. Even though it was surrounded by freezing temperatures, the heat from the sun's rays caused the icicle to warm up enough to melt.

Then came the application for my life. No matter how hostile the environment may be, including other people's cold cruelty and indifference, I can choose to dwell in the bright presence of God's loving Son. If I make that choice, I will have a warm and merry heart, even if no one else around me experiences that.

My joy is not dependent on what others say or do to me. He will give me joy! He will give you joy too, if you choose to stay in His presence.

Thou wilt show me the path of life; in thy presence is fullness of joy; at thy right hand there are pleasures for evermore.
Psalms 16:11

The Thick Fog

*B*efore she had her driver's license, Rebekah was invited to go to a party on New Year's Day, in Moses Lake, 30 miles away. She really wanted to go and I had agreed to drive her. When we took off there was a little fog, but nothing too serious. We enjoyed a good visit on the drive.

It was on my return trip back home alone that the fog became so thick I really couldn't see much beyond my front bumper. I was white-knuckle driving and really becoming afraid of what might be on the road ahead of me. I kept wondering if I could see far enough ahead to stop, if needed. I was just creeping along. It was going to take over three hours to get home at that rate.

Of course I was praying for safety and guidance. I was praying out loud fervently and continuously. I was also wondering if I should just pull over and wait out the fog, but that idea made me wonder if I'd be rear-ended, since the shoulder of the road was quite narrow.

Then God so calmly instructed me. "This drive home is so much like life in general. You really can't see what all's ahead, but you do *not* have to be afraid. You *must* put your trust in Me. Trust that I will make you to know what you need to do, in time to do it. Then relax and enjoy Me."

That's just what I did. I put my trust in the One who sees everything. I believed that He would guide me home and make me to know if I needed to stop, or anything else. I relaxed my fierce grip on the steering wheel. Instead of nervously praying, I sang songs of love and gratitude to Him all the way home. I arrived home safely and much wiser!

For [God] *looketh to the ends of the earth, and seeth under the whole heaven; to make the weight for the winds; and He weigheth the waters by measure.*
Job 28:24-25

Rich Man Poor Man

*O*he Sunday morning the Lord God Almighty instructed me to share this parable with a congregation in Quincy, Washington that was struggling with their finances.

I was to ask them to imagine that a poor, homeless man, without a job came to this church and said, "I want to donate several hundred thousand dollars for your building fund." Of course there wouldn't be much hope or expectation that he could do what he had said.

Now, what if Bill Gates, the Washington billionaire, was to walk in and make the same offer? There would probably be cheers and shouts of joy and great expectation. Bill Gates could easily come up with that kind of money.

Then the Lord instructed me to challenge the congregation, "Why the difference in those two reactions?"

Obviously, the difference is that people believe the rich man will come through. Well, God is richer than the richest man on earth. Therefore we, as Believers, ought to be reading His Word, the Bible, and allowing His Holy Spirit to quicken verses to us.

When He does quicken His Word, we had better not treat His words like the homeless beggar's words. The King of kings and Lord of lords deserves to be treated with integrity.

He says what He means. He means what He says. He has the power to do everything that He says. That deserves a shout of joy and expectation!

[Abraham] *staggered not at the promise of God through unbelief; but was strong in faith, giving glory to God. And being fully persuaded that, what* [God] *had promised, He was able also to perform.*
Romans 4:20-21

No More Snoring

It's a wonder how I came to have the book, Natural Cures "They" Don't Want You to Know About. While making my bed one morning, the Lord impressed upon me to turn on the TV, so I did. I rarely turn on the TV, especially in the morning. I had no idea what would be on, but I was certain that there was something that God wanted me to see.

An interview was in progress with Kevin Trudeau, the author of the book. Again I felt the definite urging of God's Holy Spirit instructing me to order that book. So I did. I was wondering if it might be something to help friends who were battling different health issues, since my husband, Leigh, and I weren't having any health problems, or so I thought.

When the book arrived, I was browsing through it when I saw a section on snoring. Well, we *were* having an issue with Leigh's loud snoring waking me up every night! Since he had to go to work and I stayed home, I could nap if I needed to, so we had fallen into a pattern that I didn't like.

For several weeks, I'd been getting up when his snoring woke me between 2 and 4 a.m. I'd read, or clean, or do something to stay busy and quiet until he woke up. Then after we'd have breakfast, he would leave for work, and I would head back to bed to sleep for several hours. I didn't like sleeping away my mornings, but I was too tired to stay awake. We'd been wondering about Leigh having surgery or something to stop the snoring.

Then I read the simple natural solution—drink more water. Most snoring is usually caused by dehydration. Before that I had often asked Leigh if he was getting enough water, since I rarely saw him drinking any. He had assured me that he was drinking plenty. However, that evening I asked Leigh to drink a glass of water every hour before we went to bed. He did, and lo and behold, there was no snoring that night!

Now we make sure he has several glasses of water in the evening and we put a huge glass of water on our headboard. If he wakes me up by snoring, I simply ask him to please drink some water. He does, and we both go back to sleep.

There is no doubt in my mind that the One who knows the number of hairs on our heads (Matthew 10:30), also cares about *everything* that affects us. He knows what we need.

He has wonderful ways of communicating to us right now, right where we are, like He did when He prompted me turn on the TV, and then to buy the book. What a great difference that book has made in our lives!

I will instruct thee and teach thee in the way which thou shalt go.
Psalms 32:8a

Cards with Bea

*B*ea came to the weekly Bible study that my husband and I were attending in 2005, in Wenatchee. When I was introduced to Bea, I felt drawn to her. She had lovely white hair and looked like Roy Rogers' wife, Dale Evens.

Bea, 85, had recently been widowed, and was very quiet. She and I had been sitting on a loveseat during the study. I knew the Lord wanted me to become a good friend to Bea.

As we were leaving I said, "Thanks, Bea, for sharing the loveseat with me. I really look forward to getting to know you better."

Then the quiet lady really gave me an emotional stiff arm. She quite clearly exclaimed. "Oh, I don't make friends quickly. It takes me a long time to make a friend and then I can be friends forever, but it takes a long time for me to make a new friend."

Point taken! I curbed some of my enthusiasm and remained friendly and open to Bea at the Bible studies. I still could feel God's leading to befriend Bea, but we didn't seem to really become any closer.

Then one summer evening a few weeks later, I had been doing a candle show in Wenatchee. It was about 9:30 p.m. I was preparing to drive home, when the Lord spoke to my spirit, "Go see Bea and ask if she would like to play cards with you."

I was quite nervous since she had made it very clear that she wasn't interested in rushing into any friendship. I didn't even know if she played cards, or, if she would still be up at that hour.

However, God's Spirit was quite persistent, so, I drove over to Bea's home and saw lights inside. I was still rather nervous as I rang her doorbell and waited for her to answer.

When Bea opened the door, I asked her through the screen door if she would like to play cards with me. For just a moment she froze, and I thought "Oh dear, I hope I haven't offended her."

Then with a huge grin, Bea opened the screen door, saying, "Come on in. I'd love to play cards! My husband, Red, and I used to play cards every night, after a wee bit of news. We'd play cards before going to bed. I haven't played cards with anyone since. It's been almost two years!"

Bea taught me to play Phase 10 and Ski-Bo. After that night, whenever I went to Wenatchee, I tried to stop and play cards with Bea. We did become very good friends.

I've led Bible studies in her home, we visit on the phone, we celebrate each other's birthdays, and we pray for each other. We've both been blessed for over nine years, all because I dared to obey God and invited Bea to play cards with me!

Trust in the LORD with all thine heart, and lean not unto thine own understanding. In all thy ways acknowledge Him and He shall direct thy paths.
Proverbs 3:5-6

Shocked Sherri

Sherri also came to our Bible study in Wenatchee. On her first visit with our group, when we were taking prayer requests, Sherri had a prayer request.

She asked, "Could you please pray for my diseases, especially my diabetes, and for my knees, and for me not to be in so much pain?"

She also explained that she had diabetes, GERD, knee problems, and several other things including weighing over 250 pounds on her 5' 5" frame.

We usually just sat in our places and prayed. However, after Sherri's request, I felt the Lord urging me to go kneel in front of her, lay my hands on her knees, and to pray earnestly for her healing. So I did.

As I knelt in front of her, I felt the Lord directing me to pray powerfully, so I did. I strongly resisted the enemy and I earnestly prayed for her healing from the top of her head to the soles of her feet and especially in her knees

I also prayed for her to be healed from the diabetes, and from all the other diseases too. I could feel the power of God's Holy Spirit as I prayed. I remember opening my eyes and looking up at Sherri and seeing such a shocked look on her face. I had really asked our Heavenly Father for so much more than she had requested.

She later told me that she wasn't quite sure what to think.

However, Sherri was interested to know more about God and His ways, so we often visited on the phone between small group meetings. She asked many questions about God, healing, faith, prayer, and other spiritual topics. I'd teach her what I knew, including not to say such things as "my diabetes," but rather to say, "I am fighting diabetes."

I would pray for her before we ended our phone calls. Every time I just encouraged her, taught her what the Bible said, and helped her to believe that her life could be so much better than she was experiencing.

After several months, she also started believing life could be better with God's help. She got a tread mill and began working out. Her knees got stronger, she lost weight, and was able to stop taking her diabetes medicine. Her breathing problems and GERD were ended. We could go for long walks. We'd walk and talk and pray together.

Over time Sherri began to understand what the Bible teaches on prayer. She bought a journal and we started writing down our prayer requests and leaving space to tell how God answered them. We really believed that God would answer our prayers and we were excited to see His answers.

Sherri is no longer shocked by powerful prayer. In fact, she is one of the strongest prayer warriors I know, with a powerful child-like faith. She earnestly prays daily for many people and things. Sherri is one of the first people I call when I need others to pray powerfully with me, or for me.

Confess your faults one to another, and pray one for another, that you may be healed. The effectual, fervent prayer of a righteous man availeth [accomplishes] *much.*
James 5:16

Quit Shadow Boxing

My good friend sighed, "If only God would do something to heal my sister from her awful depression."

We stood in the kitchen slicing fruit during her visit. At her words, God's Holy Spirit rose up within me. I handed her the small plaque hanging above my kitchen sink for her to read the powerful words:

Surely He hath borne our griefs, and carried our sorrows, He was wounded for our transgressions, He was bruised for our iniquities, The chastisement for our peace was upon Him, And with His stripes we are healed (Isaiah 53:4- 5).

"God has done something!" I answered. "In fact, He's already done enough for her healing. She has to fight the enemy, use some powerful verses like these. Also *Thou wilt show me the path of life. In thy presence is fullness of joy; at thy right hand there are pleasures for evermore* (Psalms 16:11). She could also be playing praise music 24/7, especially when she is feeling down."

"But you don't understand," replied my friend, "It's her mind. She's not strong like you."

"No, it's not *my* strength." I responded, "It's a spiritual battle. Spiritual battles need to be won using spiritual weapons. Remember how Saul would have David play soothing music and he would be calmed down?"

"Oh, yes," she agreed. Then we joined our husbands for breakfast.

After they left to continue their cross country journey, I pondered the situation of her sister's reoccurring battle with depression. God showed me an odd and tragic picture.

A man was being beaten up severely. The attacker wanted to actually destroy and kill him. The man felt the brutal blows and fierce kicks, but here's the odd part, instead of seeing the attacker for who it really was, the poor victim saw only the shadow of the attacker on the wall.

So, the victim was trying to use his last bit of strength to punch the shadow and to cover up the shadow. Of course the entire time those wasted efforts were going on, so was the life threatening attack.

Then the Lord showed me the meaning of this. The person represented the sister of my good friend, and many others. The brutal attacker was none other than the evil enemy that Jesus warned us about in John 10:10, who *comes to steal, to kill, and to destroy.* Instead of recognizing and fighting the real enemy, dark spirits of depression, despair, and hopelessness, she was wasting her time and efforts. She was blaming God, wallowing in fear, hopelessness, anger, self-pity, doubt, and a host of other useless behaviors that we have all "shadow boxed" at various times in our lives.

If we are to be serious about fighting the good fight of faith, then we *must* spiritually roll up our sleeves and *fight* with the Word that works! We need to find and learn, or at least, write down and begin to memorize the verses that apply to our situations. We must decide if we believe God means what His Word says or not

We can decide, like Abraham, "Yes, God has integrity, and I choose to believe that He really means this and He really can do this in my life," (Romans 4:20-21). *Then* we have begun to fight the fight of faith, referred to in I Timothy 6:12.

According to Webster, the definition of fight is 'to engage in conflict with.' May I ask you, who do you think we are engaging in conflict with when we are fighting the good fight of faith? It should definitely *not* be God!

Yet, far too many people act as if they are in conflict with God! They are trying very hard to persuade, convince, or beg God to do something. Then they piously leave an opening for Him by saying, "if it be Thy will." No wonder they get such feeble results.

May I suggest that when we are told in the Bible to fight the good fight of faith, we are being instructed to fight *with* God instead of against Him? It is sad that most people are unaware of who God really is and what He wants to do for them. He is glorious beyond description! What He wants for each of us is so wonderful we cannot even clearly imagine all of it! But we had better start imagining some of it, or our imaginations will be filled with awful alternatives that give us fear, despair, complacency, and a host of other things that are not pleasing to God, and not good for us.

How can I be so certain of this? Simple, II Tim 2:15 states, *Study to show thyself approved unto God, a workman that needeth not to be ashamed, rightly dividing the word of truth.* In today's language that would be something like, "Look, study the Bible as diligently as someone with a new and wonderful job would study to learn to do well for the big boss. If you study like that, you won't be confused or ashamed, you will know what God wants, you will understand what the Bible says and how it applies to your everyday life, all the time."

That was one of the first verses I learned as a new Believer in Jesus Christ. Perhaps more importantly, I have obeyed it for over forty years. God has done just what He said He would do in Hebrews11:6, He has rewarded me abundantly! One of the things that He has taught me is how to fight the good fight of faith and to win!

So, as I said earlier, we *must* find the verses that apply to any given situation. How do we find them? How about first of all by *asking* God to reveal His *perfect* will to you? Don't settle for wallowing around in His permissive will. What a waste!

Make the decision that you really are willing to believe what God says and ready to do what He wants you to do. Often there are conditions that we must meet before God will do all that He wants to do for us. Begin by deciding that God is smarter than you, so you will follow His way. That works much better than trying to convince God to go your way!

Then you begin searching for His answer, fully expecting Him to make you know His living Word that will work for you this time, according to His will. He is supernatural. He knows you completely, and He understands exactly what it will take to communicate with you. And most wonderfully, He is pleased to communicate with you, to protect you, to guide you, to deliver you from all evil, and to give you pleasures like a loving generous parent would enjoy doing for a dear obedient child.

So, you begin your *expectant* search for God's Word to fight the fight of faith by reading the Bible. Different tools are available to help you find verses about specific topics. Most Bibles have a concordance at the back, or you can buy one, with key words and pertaining verses listed. There are also sites on the internet to help you find specific topics in the Bible. You can begin by reading those pertaining verses. Sometimes, it is an excellent idea to fast desserts, or certain beverages, or food for part of your search.

Realize that God will find various ways to get His Word of truth to you, if you are really seeking. He may have someone say something that triggers the "Aha" moment when you *know* that is what God is saying to you. You may be reading something else that you didn't even realize had anything to do with the specific situation that you need to fight, and there will be just the "punch" you need. Perhaps a song or story will be used to teach you. He may drop insights or pictures and understanding into your very being. But most importantly you must be reading His Word to know what His ways are. He will show you. *Seek and ye shall find* (Matt. 7:7).

Of course, as Hebrews 11:1 explains, faith involves the things that we haven't seen yet, but we are so certain those things *will* happen that we start to act as if they are already a done deal! That's when we begin to *win* the fight. That's using faith that pleases God. II Chronicles. 16:9 says that's when the *most powerful Being* in the universe moves in to roll up His sleeve and to show Himself strong in our behalf!

I guarantee you that He doesn't waste His time shadow boxing. He goes for the real enemy and teaches you how to resist the enemy so that instead of dealing you deathly blows, the enemy will flee from you!

Submit yourselves therefore to God. Resist the devil, and he will flee from you.
James 4:7

Guests Coming

We saw the new couple sitting under an umbrella at the church picnic and I felt drawn to them. We asked to join them and they readily agreed. We had a most delightful time eating and visiting with them. They were traveling from California. He had business in the nearby area and she had joined him for the leisure times.

As we visited, I told them many of the stories written in this book about things that God had done in our lives over the years. They were rather amazed and eager to hear more. I don't know if they'd met anyone who knew God and His Word, and acted on it, like I did.

Before we left the picnic, we invited them to come spend a night at our home on their way back to California. They accepted.

Since we had actually built our home with our own hands, when most people visit our home for the first time, they want to tour our hand-built dream home. So, on the day of their arrival I was busily cleaning. As I was scrubbing the master bath toilet, my Master spoke to me.

He very clearly spoke into my spirit, "These people have seen other bigger, nicer homes than yours and cleaner homes too. But what they have *not* seen is someone who knows Me well and walks according to my Word. Rather than cleaning, spend time with Me before they come."

I put away my cleaning supplies and got out my Bible. I spent time worshipping and reading and praying.

When they arrived that evening, it was wonderful! My house was clean enough, and I was relaxed and filled with God's Holy Spirit. During the dinner and evening they asked many questions about God and what He'd done in our lives. I told true story after true story of what God had done in our lives.

They learned about a living, powerful, and loving God. I learned that if I really want to bless my guests, it's important to be like Mary, who sat at Jesus' feet and listened to Him, instead of Martha, who was too busy.

And Jesus answered and said unto her, Martha, Martha, thou art anxious and troubled about many things. But one thing is needful; and Mary hath chosen that good part, which shall not be taken away from her.
Luke 10:41-42

Let's Sing

While we ate lunch at the cozy diner on a Thursday, my close friend, Beryl, confided that she was battling depression and needed prayer. So, I prayed for her.

Then I invited her to my home to go through "The Steps to Freedom in Christ" workbook by Neil Anderson. She agreed. Soon she was reading the declarations of who she was in Christ Jesus. Her countenance began to relax from the pinched frown, and her voice grew stronger.

When she left my home two hours later, she was beaming! The truth had set her free.

However, she called me the following Monday to tell me the "great sadness" was back. I decided to drive over to her home, with my Bible and favorite foot cream.

On the drive over, the Lord prompted me to sing an old hymn. All I could remember was *"bring forth the royal diadem and crown Him Lord of all."* I sang those glorious words over and over. It was my prayer.

For over an hour, I massaged Beryl's feet as I hummed the hymn. We talked about, and read, Scriptures. We both wondered about the words to the hymn I was humming. We looked up the words in her hymnal and we sang the entire hymn together before I left.

She was doing better, but still sad. As I was leaving I encouraged Beryl to play Christian praise songs, since God inhabits the praises of His people. She declined explaining that as a flight attendant for almost 40 years, the roar of engines had affected her hearing to the point that she didn't like to listen to music.

The next morning the Lord spoke into my spirit telling me to call Beryl and ask her to sing songs of praise. Singing wouldn't hurt her ears and it would help her spirit.

I wanted to be sure that it was God's idea and not my own, to prevent burdening my friend with any unnecessary thing, in her fragile condition. So, I prayed. I asked God to confirm it to me from His Word that He wanted me to call and suggest the singing. I just opened my Bible and the first verse I saw was *I will sing unto the Lord as long as I live; I will sing praise to my God while I have my being* (Ps 104:33).

I called Beryl and made the suggestion. She liked the idea but couldn't think of any songs to sing. So we sang some Bible verse choruses together, over the phone.

Later that day the Lord prompted me to call Beryl's cell phone and suggest that we sing the song based on Psalms 25, *Unto thee, O LORD, do*

I lift up my soul. O my God, I trust in thee: let me not be ashamed, let not mine enemies triumph over me.

When I called her, she didn't answer. The Holy Spirit urged, "Sing the song to her voice mail."

I sang both verses, even though I don't like to sing out loud in front of anyone. Later that day she called me. She was laughing and delighted that I had sung to her! She had played it over and over.

Her oldest son, Mike, had told her, "That was quite brave of Pamela, since she doesn't really have a singing voice."

He's right. I don't have a singing voice but I do have a willing spirit with an obedient heart, and that helped my friend to laugh.

The Lord showed me several verses to study with Beryl over the next several weeks. He also gave me the idea to read a chapter of Proverbs over the phone together each evening. We took turns reading the verses out loud. Slowly but steadily, my friend let the truth make her free from her great sadness. It had started with a song!

Sing unto Him, sing Psalms unto Him, talk ye of all His wonderous works.
Glory ye in His holy name; let the heart of them rejoice that seek the
LORD.
I Chronicles 16:9-10

Milking a Cow

It had seemed like such a good idea to buy an extra calf and let it nurse with the other calves since our Holstein cows produced so much milk. However, our mama cows didn't think it was such a good idea at all!

They could tell when little Maverick tried to get some milk and they'd head butt or kick him. So, our little Maverick wasn't able to nurse with the other calves that had been born here.

Thank goodness my husband, Leigh, knew how to milk a cow. He started milking our most gentle cow, Bambi, twice a day. He filled up the two-quart calf bottle and then fed Maverick from the bottle. That plan worked just fine until Leigh had an overnight, out of town business trip.

We had milking lessons before he left. It is so much trickier than it looks to get the milk to come out, but it seemed like I had learned how to milk Bambi. So, Leigh left town after the morning feeding.

That evening I prepared to milk Bambi all by myself. I got some extra food out for her. Then I got the bottle and my stool set up beside her. She happily swished her tail and munched hay.

After about five minutes of trying to get some milk, the bottle was still empty. Bambi's extra food was almost gone and so was her patience. I was nervous. It was too late to go buy calf milk since the feed store was closed. Maverick was hungry and I obviously did *not* know how to milk a cow.

I continued to try a few more minutes and got nothing except a more disgruntled cow, which was twitching her leg and threatening to kick me. By then tears were rolling down my cheeks. I felt so helpless and I had no idea what to feed Maverick.

I stopped milking. I folded my hands, closed my eyes, and prayed, "Please, Dear God, please help me to get the milk for Maverick, in Jesus' name. Amen"

When I opened my eyes I saw how God was answering my prayer. There was a solid stream of milk spraying from one teat! I simply held the bottle under that one, and caught all the spraying milk which almost filled my two quart bottle. Then it stopped and I went to feed Maverick rejoicing that God had indeed heard and answered my prayer.

Ask, and it shall be given you; seek, and ye shall find; knock, and it shall be opened unto you;
Matthew 7:7

Torn Fabric

A long relationship is like a piece of fabric. Experiences and memories make the warp and woof. Kind words and thoughtful deeds are the beautiful patterns and designs that make each piece unique and lovely.

But what happens when the words aren't kind, the deeds aren't thoughtful? That's like tearing a piece of the fabric. What are you going to do next? Do you gasp in grief? Do you immediately examine the damage to see what can be done to repair and restore the fabric of the relationship?

Or do you ignore the tear? After all, it's not *that* big. You didn't *mean* to tear it. It won't matter, it's still just fine the way it is. So, there's no remorse that the other has been hurt and no sincere apology. Nothing is done to make restitution, and the tear remains. It's a weakened and a frayed spot that will probably get caught next time and be torn even more.

Then you have the decisions all over again. What are you going to do next? Repair the tear because the fabric is too valuable and beautiful to be ruined, or ignore it and let it continue to fray apart? Are you willing to let your heart feel the pain and do something to promote love and caring? Or are you going to harden your heart, refuse to humble yourself, and care only about yourself and what is easiest for you?

Every one of us who is married has a piece of fabric with our spouse. For some the fabric is still strong and beautiful, woven with joyful memories, mended with tears and tenderness. Its beauty is treasured and appreciated. This fabric of life is precious and cared for lovingly.

For others the poor piece is almost completely shredded by selfishness, indifference, contempt, disgust, blame, and bitterness. That piece of fabric is treated as worthless and sometimes even discarded.

We aren't talking about a hunk of material. We are talking about living hearts in relationship to each other and to the Author of life. Each family member, or friend, that comes into our lives is a very real gift from God. He knows how to make magnificent masterpieces of our lives and our relationships. He can even teach us how to repair the torn areas and transform them into beauty and grace and strength.

The choice is ours. Hard hearts tear and destroy life's fabric of relationships. Tender hearts seek God's way of lovingly guarding and repairing life's rich fabric of relationships.

Rend your heart, and not your garments, and turn unto the LORD your God, for He is gracious and merciful, slow to anger, and of great kindness.
Joel 2:13a

Cylinders of Light

*J*esus made it very clear to His followers to *"Let your light so shine before men, that they may see your good works, and glorify your Father, who is in heaven,"* (Matthew. 5:16).

I'd always thought that meant our faces shining, like Moses, after he had spent time in God's holy presence. Or perhaps it meant letting God's Holy Spirit so direct our lives, that the Light of the world, Jesus, was seen in us by others.

One sunny day, while we were flying low in our Cessna plane, the Light of the world showed me a vision about the light of men that gave yet another meaning to Jesus' instructions. From the plane, I saw several people doing many different things. Some were working, mowing their yards or washing cars. Some were walking down the street, while others were boating, swimming, and playing.

Then God showed me it's as if *everyone, everywhere,* working, playing, or resting, had a big clear cylinder around their body that went far up into the sky. The cylinders moved as the people moved. A few cylinders were filled with radiant light all the way up, others had some light part way up, and many were quite dark.

The Lord explained that when we praise, thank, and glorify Him, no matter what we are doing, we send such a brightness into the spirit realm. Angels and demons see our "cylinders" of light and so does God! It gives Him great pleasure, glory, and honor when we choose to praise and adore Him. We unmistakably radiate His glory.

I remember that He made something very clear to me. It didn't matter whether a person was changing a diaper or preaching a sermon, the cylinder was shining, or not shining, because of the love, gratitude, and praise in the person's heart and mind.

That meant that no matter what circumstances might be going on in our lives, it is still very possible for us to be bearers of light. We get the great privilege of giving God glory in the spiritual realm!

I decided then and there that I wanted my cylinder to be continually filled with light, to the glory of God. How about you?

Giving thanks unto the Father, who hath made us fit to be partakers of the inheritance of the saints in light;
Colossians 1:12

Delighting Whom?

We have had a rocky marriage. After thirty four years, I finally heard one question that was life changing for me. It could impact you too.

There we were having another heart wrenching disagreement. Then the Holy Spirit asked me, "Do you want to delight the demons and grieve God, or do you want to glorify God and destroy the works of devils?" Instantly I made the decision, "I am *through* delighting demons and grieving God."

Some of the first verses that I ever memorized were Ephesians 4:30-32, *And grieve not the Holy Spirit of God, whereby ye are sealed unto the day of redemption. Let all bitterness, and wrath, and anger, and clamor, and evil speaking, be put away from you, with all malice; And be ye kind one to another, tenderhearted, forgiving one another, even as God for Christ's sake hath forgiven you.*

From my earliest days as a Christian, I had been aware that bitterness, wrath, anger, and evil speaking grieve God and I had diligently tried to keep those far away from my mouth and my heart. It might seem like a person deserves a big dose of those things, but it just grieves God's heart. So I'd choose not to do it, for God's sake, if not the other person's sake.

When the Holy Spirit asked me that question, I realized that I also had grieved God when I became devastated by Leigh's cruelty or indifference. I had grieved God by letting panic take over and not remembering that He is able to meet all my needs for love, validation, and everything else.

Devastation and panic delight the demons, because then I am not destroying the works of the devil like Jesus wants me to, I am wallowing in them! Remember Jesus' prayer to the Father in John 17:18, *As thou hast sent me into the world, even so have I also sent them into the world.* We learn from 1 John 3:8b, *For this purpose the Son of God was manifested, that He might destroy the works of the devil.*

From then on, I purposely chose to glorify God and destroy the works of the demons, especially in my marriage. With that quality decision made, it was much easier to stay calm, to speak the truth in love to Leigh, and to not overreact or become panic stricken, no matter what he said or did.

It does glorify God and please Him when we choose to take the high road even if the words and actions of others tempt us to take the low road. Philippians 4:13 reminds us, *I can do all things through Christ which strengthens me.* I think that especially applies to delighting the Father.

Since thou wast precious in my sight, thou hast been honorable, and I have loved thee;
Isaiah 43:4a

Forgotten Glasses

*L*ast year I ordered a pair of glasses with my bifocal prescription in the entire lens so I can read or do computer work without craning my neck. It was a great idea and I love using that pair of glasses. The only problem is that I sometimes forget to use them!

It happened again just yesterday. After writing for about two hours on the computer, I swiveled my chair to get up, and there were the reading glasses right beside me on the desk!

Only this time, as I was chiding myself for forgetting them, the LORD told me that His people do that all the time with things much more important than glasses.

I asked Him, "Could You give me some examples, Father, in Jesus name?"

"Certainly," He replied, "Peace, wisdom, faith, courage, joy, love, and most of all the awareness of My presence."

Then I remembered what His Word says:

*He is our **peace*** (Ephesians 2:14).

But of Him are ye in Christ Jesus, who of God is made unto us **wisdom**, *and* **righteousness**, *and sanctification, and redemption* (I Corinthians 1:30).

*But we have the **mind of Christ*** (I Corinthians 2:16b).

*God hath dealt to every man the measure of **faith*** (Romans 12:3c).

*Wait on the Lord; be of good **courage**, and He shall strengthen thine heart. Wait, I say, on the LORD* (Psalms 27:14).

*In thy presence is fullness of **joy*** (Psalms 16:11b).

*I have loved thee with an everlasting **love*** (Jeremiah 31:3b).

*Have not I commanded thee? Be strong and of good **courage**; be not afraid, neither be thou dismayed: for the **LORD thy God is with thee** whithersoever thou goest* (Joshua 1:9).

So, let's understand that God has already provided many resources for each one of us, if we'll just remember to choose them. They have been designed by the generous and brilliant Creator who *shall supply all your need according to His riches in glory by Christ Jesus* (Philippians 4:19).

Bless the LORD, O my soul, and forget not all his benefits.
Psalms 103:2

New Year's Blessings

*A*fter our New Year's Eve party, all of our guests had either gone home or gone to bed. I was snuggled in my bed, praising and thanking God. I was enjoying His presence. As I basked in the love and peace with my Abba Daddy, He held His face so close to mine. I didn't see Him, but I felt Him. He showed me a deeper meaning to the words of the prayer that we had prayed that night with our son, Adam, when he called to wish us "Happy New Year."

Nowadays, with our adult children, we end almost every call by praying together. We all pray out loud the same prayer that we ended our nightly prayers with, each night before we went to bed, while they lived at home. It's based on Numbers 6, "The LORD bless you and keep you. The LORD make His face shine upon you. The LORD look upon you with favor and give you peace, in Jesus' name. Amen."

That night, as God's Holy Spirit enveloped me in God's love, I realized that it's very important not to say those words in the prayer too quickly or too routinely. We must let the wonderful, powerful reality of God's closeness and caring surround us, each time we pray that prayer.

It's amazing really. We are asking God to keep us, or to hold us close to Him, and He's very willing to actually do that. When we ask God to make His face shine upon us, we are asking Him to come very close and look at us with loving kindness and delight. As God looks upon us with favor, He comes very near to us as yet another intimate gesture of His pleasure! Knowing that God is that close, caring for, and delighting in us, does give us great peace, just as the prayer requests.

As I finally drifted off to sleep, I realized that the heart of God Almighty, the Heavenly Father, has always been the same towards His people—to have us simply and completely be His people and let Him be our God.

The LORD bless thee, and keep thee; The LORD make His face to shine upon thee, and be gracious unto thee; The LORD lift up His countenance upon thee, and give thee peace.
Numbers 6:24-26

The Bull's Eye

I have helped several couples through a crisis in their marriage, by giving them Biblical truths in very practical ways, and praying earnestly with them. It never ceases to amaze me how God will awaken me, usually very early in the morning, to show me Bible verses that are exactly what will help the couple to see the problem in a different light. Then they can do something to improve the situation. He also often shows me parables to help me teach His truths.

In one phone conversation with a couple in conflict crisis, the wife reacted to words from her husband about the children in their blended family. She broke into tears and ran away from the phone. The husband and I talked a little more. I encouraged him to have his son give the stepmom a "home run apology" [See pp.80-81]. He agreed to do that.

I called the wife the next day to share the verses that God brought to my mind when He had awakened me early that morning. She told me about the latest round in their situation.

Her husband had asked his son to apologize to her, the stepmom. Unfortunately, the stepmom, who was struggling with perfectionist strongholds, hadn't felt like the timing was right. The apology hadn't seemed sincere enough, and for several other important-to-her reasons, the whole event had been very painful to her. She had reacted angrily and that had triggered her husband to also react angrily. Needless to say, the stepson was also hurt and angry.

Just then the Lord showed me a picture that helped that couple and I believe it will help others also. It was as if the wife was carrying around a large poster board in front of her with a target on it. The target represented her heart. The center of the target had a very small bull's eye opening.

That tiny bull's eye on the target represented how someone could touch her heart deeply. The problem was that even though the poster board target was about 2 by 3 feet large, the bull's eye opening was only the size of a pin hole.

What an incredibly small opening to allow anyone to give her love, acceptance, compassion and significance! Any effort that missed the bull's eye was considered totally unacceptable. It had completely missed the mark, as far as she was concerned. She wasn't able to receive anything good from it.

The Lord made it clear that we all carry around such "targets" and we get to cut the opening for the bull's eye whatever size we choose. The problem is that we can make the opening so narrowly focused, too specific, and demand perfection. Then we've made it almost impossible for others to reach our heart. We suffer while others lose the joy of really connecting with, and meeting, someone else's deep needs of the heart. A tiny bull's eye means everyone misses out on love.

I encouraged the wife to cut the bull's eye opening as large as she could and be ready to accept and appreciate any and all attempts to be kind and considerate of her. I explained that her gracious appreciation and genuine thankfulness for anything that even came towards the "bull's eye" encouraged her family to aim more good things, more often, at her heart's "target."

What size is your heart target's bull's eye?

Put on therefore, as the elect of God, holy and beloved, tender mercies, kindness, humbleness of mind, meekness, longsuffering; Forbearing one another, and forgiving one another, if any man have a quarrel against any, even as Christ forgave you, so also do ye. And above all these things put on love, which is the bond of perfectness.
Colossians 3:12-14

God Sang!

In 2004, I earned a trip to the Bahamas, from selling candles. On the awards night, my husband became very mean-spirited and bitter towards me. I went to the pool to swim laps and heal. While I swam, I sang in my mind the chorus from a wonderful song that I had recently heard, "The Power of Your Love," by Geoff Bullock. Those lyrics, especially the chorus really lifted my spirit, and after about 30 minutes of swimming and singing, I could face the evening.

Here are some lyrics and the chorus, used with permission from Geoff Bullock:

> "Lord I come to You, Let my heart be changed, renewed. Hold me close, Let Your love surround me, Bring me near, Draw me to Your side, And as I wait I'll rise up like the eagle, And I will soar with You, Your Spirit leads me on, by the power of Your love."

Several months later, as I was driving to do a candle show in Republic, Washington, about 3½ hours away, the most amazing thing happened. I was thanking and praising God for helping me that time in the Bahamas.

Then suddenly and clearly, in my mind or spirit, a deep rich male voice started singing the chorus to me, only He changed the words to:

> "I'll hold you close, Let My love surround you, Bring you near, Draw you to My side, and as you wait, you'll rise up like the eagle, and you will soar with Me, My Spirit leads you on, by the power of My love."

He sang to me the *entire* trip! The 3½ hours seemed like it took less than 30 minutes. It was so majestic, personal, and uplifting. That was one of the most holy times that I've ever experienced. But there's more!

Last night, June 25, 2012, was another night that my husband was again being mean-spirited and bitter towards me. As I fell asleep I remembered the time, eight years ago that I sang to God in the pool and then He sang to me in the car, *but I couldn't remember the words, or the song.*

So, I prayed before falling asleep. I asked God if He would please remind me of that beautiful song, even though I hadn't heard it for so many years. He asked if I would start writing my book again, if He told me the song's title.

I hadn't written for several months, but I quickly answered, "Yes, I will write about it by the day after You tell me the song."

I fell asleep, slept peacefully, and woke up at 5:30 a.m. this morning. I turned on the radio to a different Christian station than usual, thinking I would rather listen to music than talking.

They were playing beautiful praise music. I lay in bed praising God with all my heart. After about 20 minutes *the* song came on, "By the Power of Your Love," by Geoff Bullock!

Isn't God wonderfully amazing? And today I began writing again.

The LORD, thy God, in the midst of thee is mighty; He will save, He will rejoice over thee with joy; He will rest in His love, He will joy over thee with singing.
Zephaniah 3:17

Staph Stopped

Two important things happened when our son, Adam, came home for Christmas break during his senior year of college. The first was that we prayed for the athlete's foot that he'd contracted in the dorm and God healed him. The second thing was that Adam attended the Bible study with us where we were learning in Galatians and Deuteronomy about Jesus redeeming us from the curse.

Adam came home for Spring Break that year on a Saturday. He told me that he had athlete's foot again and asked me to pray for him. As I reached for his foot, I was stunned! Whatever he had was *not* merely athlete's foot. He had a big red blotch behind his right knee and his entire lower leg was swollen to about twice its normal size. It was a deep purple color with streaks of red and there were dark oozing cracks in his skin.

I said, "We need to get you to a doctor." Off we raced to the walk-in clinic in nearby Moses Lake. There the doctor informed us that Adam had a very serious case of staph infection! The doctor gave Adam a shot, prescribed antibiotics, and warned us that if he wasn't better by Monday, he would be hospitalized and amputation may be needed!

Needless to say, we began praying for the staph to be healed. We got the prescription and gave it as directed. I anointed Adam with oil. We made a make-shift bed on the living room floor so that Adam could keep his leg elevated up on the couch. I changed the sheets both morning and evening. He ate only very healthy food, absolutely no sugar. I fasted.

My husband, Leigh, got home Sunday. He also fasted and prayed. We asked others to be praying for Adam's healing. We played praise music. We knew it is written *He sent His word, and healed them, and delivered them from their destructions* (Psalms 107:20). So, we played CD's that read the Bible to us continually, even in Adam's sleep. We only spoke positive words, nothing negative and absolutely no strife (James 3:16).

I still remember how shocked and sickened I felt when I checked Adam on Monday morning and found that the red streaks had shot beyond his legs, up into his armpits and even into his neck and face! I called the doctor's office and made an appointment for that afternoon.

I was wondering what else we could do to fight the staph as I was walking into the living room to tell Adam what time the appointment would be. Then God's Word broke into the situation! Strongly and clearly the Holy Spirit spoke to me, "Read Deuteronomy 28." I grabbed my Bible and told Adam, "God has something for us in Deuteronomy 28!"

I began reading Deuteronomy 28 out loud to Adam. The first fourteen verses describe the blessings that God will send to His obedient people.

The rest of the chapter details the curses that will come upon the disobedient. The Holy Spirit rose up within me when I read verse 35, *The LORD shall smite thee in the knees, and in the legs, with a sore botch that cannot be healed, from the sole of thy foot unto the top of thy head.*

That curse exactly described what we were dealing with and I knew that Adam had been redeemed from those curses by Jesus Christ when He hung on the cross. That's what we had studied at Christmas time!

So I read Galatians 3:13-14 out loud. *Christ hath redeemed us from the curse of the law, being made a curse for us; for it is written, Cursed is every one that hangeth on a tree:* [the original word means wood, like the cross!] *That the blessing of Abraham might come on the Gentiles through Jesus Christ; that we might receive the promise of the Spirit through faith.*

Next I read Galatians 3:26-27 and 29 out loud. *For ye are all the children of God by faith in Christ Jesus. For as many of you as have been baptized into Christ have put on Christ. And if ye be Christ's, then are ye Abraham's seed, and heirs according to the promise.*

With God's Word energizing my spirit, I laid my hands on Adam's leg and I boldly prayed, "Glory to God! Thank you that Adam has been redeemed by Jesus Christ from the curse of this blotch in his knees that cannot be healed from the sole of his foot to his head! I resist this curse in Jesus' holy name! Let there be the healing that God Almighty wants for Adam, in Jesus' holy name! Amen."

When I opened my eyes, I saw God do a miracle! The dark purple and dark red color on Adam's legs faded before our eyes into light pink and even patches of normal colored skin! The streaks up into his upper body disappeared! Boy, did we praise God! Then I called the doctor's office and cancelled the appointment.

We continued with all the healthy things that we had been doing and we praised God as He continued to completely heal Adam. His body looked normal, except that you could still see some discoloration where the oozing cracks had been. By the end of the week, Adam drove his car eight hours back to his university in Montana without any pain or trouble.

The doctor had advised Adam to go to the campus doctor when the antibiotics were used up to be checked again. So, he did. They performed two different blood tests to be certain that he was healed because they could still see some of the discoloration and could tell that it had been a very serious thing. Praise the Lord! Both tests came out clean. God had stopped the staph and Adam had been completely healed!

Then they cry unto the LORD in their trouble, and He saveth them out of their distresses. He sent His word, and healed them, and delivered them from their destructions.
Psalms 107:19-20

A Thumb View

*G*od made me aware of a struggle that most of us are engaged in, even if we're unaware of it. Whether we understand it or not, we are involved in a very serious spiritual battle. We will lose if we don't really see the truth in the struggle with the facts. It's an example of what God's Word states in Hosea 4:6a, *My people are destroyed for lack of knowledge: because thou hast rejected knowledge, I will also reject thee.*

In my spirit I could sense that it was as if God was offering this wonderful gift that He wanted for His people. Yet instead of beholding the beautiful gift that God has for them, most people see something else entirely different. I was wondering if God would help me see it as a picture. He did that, quite literally.

He showed me it was as if God was bringing the most beautiful glowing painting in a gorgeous frame to one of His children. The picture represented their heart's desire in God's perfect will and it was breathtaking in a way that only God could do. Nevertheless, instead of viewing the picture with awe and thanksgiving, the person was holding up their thumb very close to one eye and the other eye was closed.

The close up view of the thumb completely blocked the view of the gorgeous big picture. They couldn't see God's perfect will. They couldn't see the truth in God's Word for them.

Let's think about truth and facts for a moment. God's Word is truth. Jesus made that very clear in John 17:17, *Sanctify them through thy truth; thy word is truth.*

Our situation is a fact. The symptom of a disease is a fact or our bank statement is a fact. The thumb in front of our eye is a fact.

Now here is the interesting thing in all of this. If you concentrate on the fact, you will just continue to experience the fact, and probably nothing else will change. Even if it did start to change, you would be so preoccupied with the problem, or the fact, or the thumb in front of your eye, that you might not even realize something wonderful was happening.

God does have a wonderful plan and picture for your life. Since the thumb view blocks the view of God's plan, let's agree that the thumb view is the dumb view.

However, if you view the *truth,* or what God says about the situation, you will see that the truth in God's Word is powerful enough to put the fact in perspective. The truth, combined with faith, is even powerful enough to change the facts to line up with the truth of God's Word.

The amazing and holy thing is that God's Word is mysteriously self-energizing. It has living power to become what God sent it to do. That's what God is telling us in Isaiah 55:11, *So shall my word be that goeth forth out of my mouth; it shall not return unto me void, but it shall accomplish that which I please, and prosper in the thing whereto I sent it.*

So, I encourage you, no matter what situation is looming so large in your life, go to God's Word. Then ask Him to show you what He has to say about it. Choose to focus on the truth that God says about your facts or situation.

Then every time the thought of the situation comes to your mind, repeat the truth from God's Word and expectantly watch for Him to do what He said He would do. Stop focusing on the thumb view.

[Abraham] *staggered not at the promise of God through unbelief, but was strong in faith, giving glory to God; and being fully persuaded that, what* [God] *had promised,* [God] *was able also to perform.*
Romans 4:20-21

Ocean Waves

As I sat by the Puget Sound listening to the waves gently roll to the shore, the Lord revealed this picture to me about experiencing the reality of His Word.

It's as if His Word is the entire ocean. The part that I am really experiencing the most is the current wave that I am standing in, or floating on.

It's one thing to just gaze at the sea, or the Bible, and say "Yes, that's the ocean," or "Yes, that's God's Word." How much more refreshing and personal it is to actually get into the ocean, or the Bible, and really experience it!

God's heart longs to refresh us, lift us, comfort us, and intimately touch us, as we read His Word. Let's be searching the Bible for a word, like a wave, to ride on or to stand in. That's how we experience the reality that God's Word works!

And they were all amazed, and spake among themselves, saying, What a word is this!
Luke 4:36a

Bougainvillea

My bougainvillea plant is over eight feet tall. With its lush leaves and profuse delicate pink blossoms, it is my favorite among all my many plants, when it is blooming. The only problem is that it dries out very easily and then it can become an eyesore of tangled unsightly branches with brown crispy leaves.

Trimming those dead branches is no easy chore because along with the delicate pink blossoms, the branches also produce sharp thorns over ½ inches long. Those thorns do not get any duller when the branch dies. So it is a real chore to trim the plant.

One day when I was bemoaning the need to trim a large section of the bougainvillea, I noticed on the other side of the plant, a lush section of green leaves and a beautiful bouquet of pink blossoms. I decided to turn the plant around so that I could see the lush side. Then its beauty inspired me to trim out the ugly parts. That's when the Lord spoke to my heart.

He showed me that in life we all have areas that need some painstaking work. He helped me understand how valuable it is to focus on the good and beautiful parts, and also to be willing to work on the needy parts.

I sometimes tend to think something is worthless before it really is. Now I try to see if there's a bouquet hiding somewhere, even among thorns.

Finally, brethren, whatever things are true, whatever things are honest, whatever things are just, whatever things are pure, whatever things are lovely, whatever things are of good report; if there be any virtue, and if there be any praise, think on these things.
Philippians 4:8

Niagara Falls

*P*roverbs 3:5-6 teaches, *Trust in the LORD with all thine heart; and lean not unto thine own understanding. In all thy ways acknowledge Him, and He shall direct thy paths.* That is exactly what I've tried to do in my life. One of the many areas that the LORD has directed in wonderful ways is my traveling. He directed some amazing things for me to see Niagara Falls and to go on a cruise, both of which had been desires of my heart.

The path to Niagara Falls actually started almost one year before I saw the Falls. In 2002, my husband, Leigh, and I were blessed to fly to Hawaii to enjoy a trip I'd earned from my candle sales. Our return flight was overbooked so we gave up our seats in exchange for two free passes on that airline. We flew home later that night.

When I got home, I was blessed selling candles and earned the next incentive trip which was a Caribbean cruise for May, 2003. That was another heart's desire, to go on a romantic cruise with Leigh. I was excited and thankful about the cruise. I wasn't thinking about making any other travel plans. Amazingly, God had other plans.

One afternoon about a month before we were to set sail, God's Holy Spirit spoke to me, "You'd better check the date on the free passes you have. They expire sooner than you think."

Sure enough, the passes were only good for one more month! I called Leigh and we decided it might be great to fly to Kansas to see our friends, Craig and Suzanne.

Before I called the airlines, I did what has become my habit before making trip plans; I bowed my head and prayed for God's perfect will to be done. When I called the airlines to book the flight, I learned that they don't fly to Kansas.

Then Leigh and I thought about San Diego, but again that was not an option for those passes. We couldn't fly south. I asked, "Where do you fly that I can use these passes?"

The agent mentioned a few places, including Toronto where I could see Niagara Falls. That sounded great to me. I excitedly told her, "I'll check with my husband and call you right back."

Leigh agreed and we found a free weekend two weeks before the cruise. I eagerly called back on the same airline reservation number that I had just been using, ready to book our flight to Toronto.

At first I was exasperated when a different agent informed me that I *couldn't* use the passes to fly to Toronto. Then I remembered that I had asked God for His perfect will.

I just truthfully said, "Oh dear, I was so looking forward to seeing Niagara Falls."

"Well then, you could use these passes to fly to Buffalo, New York and drive to see Niagara Falls," she said, "It's not very far."

That's just what we did. Since the flight was free, we decided to splurge and booked a gorgeous room for our two nights overlooking Niagara Falls from the Canadian side.

Our flight to Buffalo had a layover in Minneapolis. During the first leg of the flight I was in the process of reading through The Message Bible for my first time. I kept reading the phrase God of the Angel Armies (Psalms 24:10). I asked the lady beside me, who I'd learned was also a Believer, what words she thought the King James Version used for that phrase. Neither of us knew.

I had just finished reading Psalms 37:39-40 in The Message, *The spacious, free life is from GOD, it's also protected and safe. GOD-strengthened, we're delivered from evil—when we run to him, he saves us.*

The crew made an announcement that our flight was being delayed into Minneapolis. I knew that our connecting flight to Buffalo was the last flight out that day. So, if we missed it, we'd be stuck in Minneapolis and be paying for, but not staying at, our beautiful room in Canada that had a 72 hour cancellation policy! It was too late to cancel that night's reservation.

I knew that in the whole scheme of world events, the hotel situation wasn't exactly evil, but at that moment in my life it seemed like evil and I'd just read that we are delivered from evil. So, I bowed my head, praying to God, asking Him to deliver me from this "evil" of not getting to stay at the hotel, even though we'd paid for that night.

He taught me quite a lesson in prayer! He said, "Well, you just prayed for a safe trip today. It will be a safe trip. You didn't pray for anything more specific."

Then and there, I earnestly and *specifically* prayed, "Dear Heavenly Father, God of the Angel Armies, Would You please help us get to Niagara Falls while it is still called today? Could we please stay in our beautiful room that we've already paid for, in Jesus' holy name? Amen."

Leigh and I made a plan for when our plane landed in Minneapolis. I was to dash out and get to the gate to see if they would hold it for Leigh to get there with our carry-on luggage. I continued reading The Message Bible. I was eager to see what my God would do.

When we landed, even though I had been over half way back in coach, I was at the exit door before any of the first class passengers even had time to standup. I dashed into the terminal only to find out I'd raced into a dead end lounge! (I often truthfully tell people that I know the way to heaven, but everything else is sketchy.)

I quickly retraced my steps and found our next gate. Sure enough they were willing to wait for Leigh, who arrived a short time later with our carry-ons. We were thankful that we only had carry-ons for that trip.

On our flight to Buffalo I was so overjoyed by what God had done for us. I continued to read the Message, praising God for delivering us from evil. Little did I know that it wasn't over, yet!

At the car rental counter in Buffalo, there was the slowest, most unhelpful agent that I had ever seen. We were third in line. The agent took over half an hour just reading all the fine print to the man at the counter and she seemed to delight in telling him all the restrictions. When the lady in front of us got her turn, she angrily complained to the agent about how slow and unkind she had been. That only made the agent go slower with her car rental.

I kept specifically praying that we could please see Niagara Falls while it is still called today. When it was our turn, I smiled at the agent and silently prayed for her. Amazingly, she had our car ready fairly fast.

On to the next hurdle. There was road construction on the way to our hotel and we got lost. Somehow, in the dark, without any signs, on roads that were all torn up, Leigh got us to our hotel!

We dashed in. I asked the concierge, "Can we really see Niagara Falls from our room?"

"Oh, yes," he said, "It's right out those windows."

Even though it was a lovely five-star hotel, I dashed across the lobby and put my face to the glass like a kid at a candy store. Peering out I saw the most gorgeous view of colored lights on the majestically cascading waterfall. Then, in a moment it all went black!

"What happened?" I asked.

"The lights go out at midnight," he calmly replied.

Then the full force of my answered prayer hit me! God, the God of the Angel Armies, my Heavenly Father, who cares and answers prayer, had indeed gotten us to Niagara Falls while it was still called today!

I was so awed by God that I practically floated up to our room. It was really a magnificent place with a fireplace at the foot of the elegant and comfortable bed. In the bathroom there was a huge tub and shutters that opened to a view of Niagara Falls.

A comfy chair sat by the window also directly looking over Niagara Falls. That's where I was sitting early the next morning. I was surprised to see that Niagara Falls was even larger than I had seen the night before, while the lights were being shut off.

I was praising God, beholding the breath-taking beauty, and blinking back tears of joy when God spoke to me, "I am like Niagara Falls in that I am so much more than most people see, especially if they only take a quick glance."

I continued to praise Him and behold the beauty. It was such an answer to prayer and a desire of my heart to get to be there. I was basking in the spacious, free life from God, just like I'd read in the Message Bible.

Amazingly, there is one more thing that God did to deliver us from evil and to keep us protected and safe on that trip. We didn't even realize what He had done until we were getting ready to go on the cruise two weeks later.

2003 was the year that Toronto had the SARS outbreak and epidemic. The cruise ship was posting notices that anyone who had been to Toronto within the last several weeks would *not* be allowed to board the ship. If we had actually booked our flight into Toronto, as the one agent recommended, we would have been excluded from the cruise!

Praise God, the God of the Angel Armies, or as the KJV states, the Lord of Hosts for protecting and blessing us!

Who is this King of glory? The LORD of hosts, He is the King of glory.
Psalms 24:10

Whirligig of Sin

*O*ur daughter, Rebekah, was being very tempted to be squeezed into the world's way of living when God showed me this parable to tell to her. I saw a park that represented our lives. In the park was a playground whirligig, a big metal spinning plate with handrail bars radiating out from the center to the edges. Several people can stand on it and hang on while someone on the ground grabs hold of it and runs to make the it spin, delighting those riding the whirligig.

Being raised in a Christian home, Rebekah grew up hearing and obeying the warnings to stay away from the whirligig of sin. But as she grew into a young adult, she was enticed by the sounds of the people on the whirligig laughing and acting like they were having such a fun time. After all, it didn't exactly look evil.

In the parable picture, since it was only going around slowly, Rebekah was tempted to step up on the whirligig and take a very short ride. She did. Lo and behold, she found that she could jump off when she wanted and she didn't seem to be hurt or dizzy.

Then God showed me how sin is like that whirligig ride. In the beginning it can seem fun. We think we can just stop when we want. However, sooner or later, and often, without even really realizing how fast it's spinning, a rider will discover that the whirligig is zipping around way too fast to get off without being hurt quite badly.

The rider knows she's getting dizzy and feeling sick, but she's also afraid to jump off. Then the rider is caught in the trap of sin, even though it is destructive. The sorry rider learns that it is harder to stop than she ever realized it would be. Some people never even get off the whirligig of sin, they just move closer to the center and stay stuck on it all their lives.

By far, the best choice is to stay away from the whirligig of sin, that's what II Timothy 2:22a warns us, *"Flee also youthful lusts."*

We need to be aware that sin often appears as delightful and quite harmless. However, if we know and obey God's Word, we won't be deceived by the seemingly fun pleasure of the whirligig of sin!

By faith, Moses, when he was come to years, refused to be called the son of Pharaoh's daughter; choosing rather to suffer affliction with the people of God, than to enjoy the pleasures of sin for a season.
Hebrews 11:24-25

Thirsty Cows

God showed me something using our very thirsty cows, when I went outside to water the daffodils along the driveway. Our two mama cows saw me and began mooing in a way that I have come to recognize as meaning, "We have a big problem, we really need help."

I realized that their water barrel was empty. We keep a 55 gallon barrel in their pasture with an automatic self-filler. Lately, the self-filler hadn't shut off, so it made a messy flood. We'd found it much cleaner to just turn on the water each day to fill the barrel, then shut the water off.

Heading to the faucet to turn on the water for them, I went out of their sight. Their moo changed to their panic cry, which is a much higher and longer moo, almost a trumpet blast. That's when the Lord showed me what people do so often to Him.

We can be just like the cows which became panicked when they couldn't see me, even though I was doing the very thing that would solve their problem So too with people who are praying.

Too often, after someone has asked God for something, while He is in the very act of fulfilling the request, instead of waiting patiently, expectantly thankful that God is taking care of the request, the petitioner, turns very panicky and frantic. That does not show faith or trust in the One being asked to help.

Next time we ask God for something that we know is His will, let's not be like the cows who trumpet their panic. Let's be trustful and wait expectantly for God to answer our prayers according to His Word and His character.

Soon, the water sloshed into the barrel. After both cows had gulped gallons of water, they began their low mooing which I think means, "Thank you, we are very content."

That would be a good thing for us to say to God too. Let's not forget to thank Him for His answers and provisions. How much greater it would be if we did that, even while waiting for the answer!

The LORD is my rock, and my fortress, and my deliverer; my God, my strength, in whom I will trust; my shield, and the horn of my salvation, and my high tower.
Psalms 18:2

God's 1, 2, 3 Plan

There's an important pattern the Lord showed me. I call it the divine love story of God's 1, 2, 3 plan, because there are three phases to it. In the first phase, God gets us out of bondage. In the second phase, He draws us unto Himself. In the third phase, God lavishes His presence and His blessings upon us, including victory over our enemies.

The interesting thing about this plan is that it must happen in this order. If we are not removed from bondage, it is impossible to be close to God. If we aren't close to God, by that I mean worshiping Him and obeying Him, then we will worship the blessings.

If we worship *anything*, besides the Lord God Almighty and His Son, Jesus Christ, that thing will put us in bondage! Without phases 1 and 2 being accomplished in our lives, the great blessings would just become bondage for us.

That's why the very first commandment of the Ten that God gave Moses was to put God first. Exodus 20:1-3 powerfully states, *And God spake all these words, saying. I am the LORD thy God, which have brought thee out of the land of Egypt, out of the house of bondage. Thou shalt have no other gods before me.*

We must not worship knowledge, wealth, health, family, organizations, fame, power, pleasure, or anything else. God desires to be our highest priority and greatest love. When He is that to us, He does lavish good things on us, because God is love and love gives (I John 4:8).

We can enjoy those good gifts in their rightful place. So, from Genesis to Revelation God reveals His love story 1, 2, 3 plan, His heart's great desire, is to have us be His people and for Him to be our God!

You can easily see that plan with Abraham. In Genesis 12:1 God called him out of bondage in his father's country filled with traditions and ungodly culture, *Now the LORD had said unto* [Abraham] *Get thee out of thy country, and from thy kindred, and from thy father's house, unto a land that I will show thee.*

By Genesis 12:7, the LORD appeared to Abraham, who was still known as Abram, and promised to give him much land with descendants to fill it. Abraham did two important things. He worshipped God by building an altar and Abraham obeyed God. So he kept moving and pitching his tent wherever God led him.

God continued to draw Abraham to Himself and in Genesis 15:1 we learn, *After these things the word of the LORD came unto* [Abraham] *in a vision. Saying Fear not, I am thy shield, and thy exceeding great reward.*

By Genesis 18, Abraham was learning that nothing is too hard for the LORD! By then God was revealing His plans to Abraham and Abraham was boldly asking God for things.

A king gave generous gifts to Abraham in Genesis 20:14 to make peace with him. By Genesis 23:6, the neighbors called Abraham, *my lord, thou art a mighty prince among us.*

Truly God kept His promise of Genesis 12:2 to Abraham, *And I will make of thee a great nation, and I will bless thee, and make thy name great, and thou shalt be a blessing.* God followed His 1, 2, 3 plan.

Then God did it again for Abraham's son, Isaac. We see all three phases described by God in Genesis 26:2-3a, *And the LORD appeared unto* [Isaac], *and said, Go not down into Egypt* [Egypt represents bondage in the Old Testament]; *dwell in the land which I shall tell thee of: Sojourn in this land and I will be with thee, and will bless thee.*

Isaac obeyed and followed God whole heartedly. Some of Isaac's blessings are described in Genesis 26:12-13, *Then Isaac sowed in that land, and received in the same year an hundredfold: and the LORD blessed him. And the man waxed great, and went forward, and grew until he became very great.*

The wonderful thing is that Isaac continued to really worship and be surrendered to God as we see in Genesis 26:24-25, *And the LORD appeared unto* [Isaac] *that same night, and said, I am the God of Abraham thy father: fear not, for I am with thee, and will bless thee, and multiply thy seed for my servant Abraham's sake. And* [Isaac] *builded an altar there, and called upon the name of the LORD, and pitched his tent there.*

Isaac's son, Jacob, also experienced the three step plan of God. In Genesis 28:1-2, God directs Jacob via his father, Isaac, who told Jacob not to take a heathen wife, which is another symbol of bondage in the Bible.

Isaac also told Jacob to go to Padanaram, to his mother's relatives, to find a godly wife. Jacob obeyed. Enroute he had quite an encounter with the living God in a dream.

God told Jacob, *behold, I am with thee, and will keep thee in all places whither thou goest, and will bring thee again into this land, for I will not leave thee until I have done that which I have spoken to thee of* (Genesis 28:15). Jacob awoke and worshipped God.

God blessed Jacob so mightily that years later when Jacob was returning to see his brother, Jacob sent ahead of his family, a gift of animals to his brother (Genesis 32:14-15). In today's market that gift would be well worth over $50,000.

Then Jacob experienced the greatest blessing of all, favor with God. God changed Jacob's name to Israel in Genesis 32:28, [God] *said, Thy*

name shall be called no more Jacob, but Israel; for as a prince hast thou power with God, and with men and hast prevailed.
Israel means a prince of God. Jacob had seen the face of God and lived! He became the mighty prince and patriarch of the nation of Israel.

God also had the 1, 2, 3 plan for the Israelites in the Old Testament. First God got them out of Egypt, a place of severe bondage for them. Then He relentlessly worked with them for 40 years to get them to believe Him and follow Him, and finally they got to go into the Promised Land.

In Leviticus 11:45, God sums it up. *For I am the LORD that bringeth you up out of the land of Egypt, to be your God: ye shall therefore be holy for I am holy.*

Unfortunately most of the Old Testament records the ways that the Israelites kept returning to bondage by putting other things, or people, before God in their hearts and lives. God patiently kept at His divine plan to deliver them and to draw them unto Himself.

Then came Jesus to pay the ultimate price to deliver us from the bondage of sin. Galatians 5:1 triumphantly encourages us to *Stand fast therefore in the liberty wherewith Christ hath made us free, and be not entangled again with the yoke of bondage.*

The divine love story continued to be demonstrated as Jesus lived and died to invite us into life with the Heavenly Father. Jesus Christ came to show us how much the Father longs for us and loves us. Then He showed us what a price they were willing to pay so that we could become children of the Most High God (Hebrews 12:2).

The New Testament abounds with page after page of the blessings that we receive from being drawn to God through Jesus Christ, His Son. The final book of the Bible, Revelation, shows the culmination of God's divine 1, 2, 3 plan.

His heart's desire is triumphantly declared in Revelation 21:3-4:

> *And I heard a great voice out of heaven saying, Behold, the tabernacle of God is with men, and He will dwell with them, and they shall be His people, and God Himself shall be with them, and be their God. And God shall wipe away all tears from their eyes; and there shall be no more death, neither sorrow, nor crying, neither shall there be any more pain: for the former things are passed away.*

Some will say that these verses I've quoted are only for the Jews. However Galatians 3:26-29 definitely explains that we are all included. We are even heirs of the promise to Abraham! *And if ye be Christ's, then are ye Abraham's seed, and heirs according to the promise* (Galatians 3:29).

As amazing as it is, the greatest Being in the universe lovingly desires to be with us. He wants to have us belong to Him and to experience what that entails. I hope you can hear the Father's heart and will joyfully participate in His great plan. He won't force any of us, but He does invite all of us!

I am the LORD, and I will bring you out from under the burdens of the Egyptians, and I will rid you out of their bondage, and I will redeem you with a stretched out arm, and with great judgments: I will take you to me for a people, and I will be to you a God: and ye shall know that I am the LORD your God... I will bring you in unto the land...I will give it to you for an heritage: I am the LORD.
Exodus 6:6b-8

Sunny Skies and Storm Clouds

*S*ome people have told me that they are really confused and frustrated trying to understand who God is and how He can be so angry in the Old Testament, and in Revelation, and then supposedly be so kind in the New Testament.

One afternoon, I was swimming in my indoor pool when God showed me something that clearly addressed that very issue. The pool is in a room about 46' long with many windows and sliding glass doors along both sides, so I have a great view of the sky while I swim and pray. Even after almost 20 years it is so remarkable to me that God gave me this pool. I'm overflowing with thanksgiving and praise every time I get in it.

That particular day, as I swam and looked to the west, the sky was a brilliant blue with a few soft puffy white clouds and sunlight shining into my windows. However, when I looked out the windows to the east it was an entirely different view. The sky was almost black, with dark grey storm clouds, and not a hint of blue sky or sunlight to be seen.

I actually looked back and forth a few times because it was such a stark difference. If I hadn't witnessed it myself, I don't think I would have believed that it was possible to be in one place looking at the sky just overhead and seeing such opposite vistas.

Then the LORD explained, "Use this example to show people how I can be so gentle and loving, yet also be so filled with wrath. Just as it's the same sky, I am the same God. Just as the different conditions result in the same sky appearing completely opposite, different conditions result in Me showing different aspects of Who I am."

Then He reminded me what His Word says:

Isaiah 40:11, [The Lord God] *shall feed His flock like a shepherd; He shall gather the lambs with His arm, and carry them in His bosom, and shall gently lead those that are with young.*

Ezekiel 5:11, 13, *Wherefore, as I live, saith the Lord God; Surely, because thou hast defiled my sanctuary with all thy detestable things, and with all thine abominations, therefore will I also diminish thee; neither shall mine eye spare, neither will I have pity. Thus shall mine anger be accomplished, and I will cause my fury to rest upon them, and I will be comforted: and they shall know that I the LORD have spoken it in my zeal, when I have accomplished my fury in them.*

Joel 2:13 Amplified Bible, *Rend your hearts and not your garments and return to the Lord, your God, for He is gracious and merciful, slow to anger, and abounding in loving-kindness; and He revokes His sentence of evil [when His conditions are met].*

Revelation 6:16-17, *And* [the people on earth] *said to the mountains and rocks, Fall on us, and hide us from the face of Him that sits on the throne, and from the wrath of the Lamb: for the great day of His wrath is come; and who shall be able to stand?*

We were created in God's image. Part of that includes our emotions, because God also has emotions. I find it amazing that people's choices can either please God, which allows Him to shower out His goodness, gentleness, and loving-kindness; or their choices can grieve God and cause His furious wrath to be manifested. He *is* the same Almighty God.

With the kind and merciful You will show Yourself kind and merciful; with an upright man You will show Yourself upright, with the pure You will show Yourself pure, and with the perverse You will show Yourself contrary.
Psalms 18:25-26 Amplified Bible

Perfect or Permissive Will

*O*ne of the most profound things that God has taught me is the difference between His perfect will and His permissive will. His perfect will is His highest, holy, best will for each of us. He also has an area where too many people operate too much of the time, in His permissive will.

His permissive will permits, or allows, everything else to happen, including ungodly things. He doesn't intervene to stop them, but it is not His best, most desired plan for us.

In the Old Testament, Balaam is an excellent example. He was a prophet summoned by an evil king's entourage to come and curse God's people, the Israelites. In Numbers 22:12, God clearly showed His perfect will, *And God said unto Balaam, Thou shalt not go with them; thou shalt not curse the people; for they are blessed.*

Instead of just obeying and walking away, Balaam, greedily desiring to go, kept talking to them, and kept trying to get God to change His mind. Finally in Numbers 22:21 *Balaam rose up in the morning, saddled his donkey, and went with the princes of Moab.*

The next verse shows us God's response. *And God's anger was kindled because* [Balaam] *went: and the angel of the LORD stood in the way for an adversary against him.*

We read God's verdict on Balaam in Jude, verse 11, *Woe unto them! For they have gone in the way of Cain, and ran greedily after the error of Balaam for reward, and perished in the gainsaying of Core.*

Of course God Almighty is brilliant and powerful. He knows everything. He can do anything. For reasons that will probably be much clearer to us in the hereafter, God has chosen to let people make their own choices. He has NOT chosen to make us puppets doing His bidding.

We can choose to obey God or choose to disobey. Both choices yield consequences. Deuteronomy 28 is a chapter dedicated to teaching us all about blessings for those who obey and curses for those who disobey. It covers a huge array of things we all encounter in our daily lives.

Jesus taught us to pray for God's perfect will. We are doing just that by praying, *Our Father which art in heaven, Hallowed be thy name. Thy kingdom come. Thy will be done, as in heaven, so in earth* (Luke 11:2).

In the New Testament we are also taught to know God's ways by studying His Word. II Timothy 2:15 gives us a key, *Study to show thyself approved unto God, a workman that needeth not to be ashamed, rightly dividing the word of truth.*

Too many times people make poor choices and then blame God for the outcome. Or they make what they think is a great choice, but they didn't bother to check with God first, they just assumed that He would bless their ideas and ways. It is so much better to check with God first, before we make our plans.

Chapter 3 in Proverbs is filled with advice about living in God's perfect will. Listen to the clear wisdom in Proverbs 3:5-8, The Message:

> *Trust God from the bottom of your heart; don't try to figure everything on your own. Listen for God's voice in everything you do, everywhere you go; He's the one who will keep you on track. Don't assume that you know it all. Run to God! Run from evil! Your body will glow with health, your very bones will vibrate with life!*

I've learned that if I don't know what His perfect will is in a situation, then I pray, "God's perfect will be done in this situation, in Jesus name."

I think that's one of the most powerful prayers that I pray.

Present your bodies, a living sacrifice, holy, acceptable unto God, which is your reasonable service. And be not conformed to this world: but be ye transformed by the renewing of your mind, that ye may prove what is that good, and acceptable, and perfect, will of God.
Romans 12:1b-2

Walking Billboards

*B*efore we had modern media, when a merchant wanted to advertise, he would hire people to walk around wearing signs with an ad. Sometimes you still see people on street corners paid to twirl signs or otherwise draw people's attention to a certain business or product.

Did you know that if you call Jesus your Lord, you are also a walking billboard for God? Other people around you are watching to see what your life is like and what your God is doing for you. Those people might be in your family, your neighborhood, your office, your church, your school, or behind you in the check-out line.

That's what Paul was referring to in II Corinthians 3:3, The Message, *Your very lives are a letter that anyone can read by just looking at you. Christ himself wrote it—not with ink, but with God's living Spirit; not chiseled into stone, but carved into human lives.*

Our words and actions shout a message to those around us. Is our message the same as the world's message? If so, we're probably speaking, and showing, fear, doubt and selfishness. Those things lead to either frantic lives trying to change something or depressed lives without hope of any change. God has a much better idea for us!

The Bible says that our lives, and our message, should be peculiar. Most of us think of peculiar as odd, but the dictionary also says peculiar can mean belonging exclusively to, or very special. So it is an honor when, in Exodus 19:5-6a, God invites us, *Now therefore, if ye will obey my voice indeed, and keep my covenant, then, ye shall be a peculiar treasure unto me above all people: for all the earth is mine: And ye shall be unto me a kingdom of priests, and an holy nation.*

The same desire of God is expressed in the New Testament, too. We are instructed in Titus 2:13-15, to be *Looking for that blessed hope, and the glorious appearing of the great God and our Saviour, Jesus Christ; Who gave Himself for us, that He might redeem us from all iniquity, and purify unto Himself a peculiar people, zealous of good works.*

Some Christians seem to cover up their signs. Very early in my Christian walk, I heard the phrase, "Don't be a Lady Clairol Christian, is she or isn't she." That was back in the day when Lady Clairol advertised that their hair coloring products were so natural and good looking, people would ask, "Does she or doesn't she?"

I decided then that I'd be glad to use Lady Clairol on my hair someday, but I didn't want there to be any doubt about my life. I wanted to be a great billboard for Jesus. I would definitely let people know that He makes a wonderful difference in my life!

So the next time we are tempted to grumble hopelessly or act selfishly, let's remember we are showing a real message. Let's proclaim the glorious truth that we were created to proclaim—I belong to a great and good God and He is for me!

But ye are a chosen generation, a royal priesthood, an holy nation, a peculiar people; that ye should show forth the praises of Him who hath called you out of darkness into His marvelous light.
I Peter 2:9

We're the Straw

During the early 1970's we had some outstanding Christian speakers come to Montana State University. One of the most profound things I ever learned came from a young, black, dynamic speaker who travelled with Campus Crusade for Christ. I don't remember his name, but I do remember his zeal. He was on fire for the Lord!

After his talk, I went forward to talk with him. I've always remembered what he said, when I praised him for doing such a great job. "I'm only the straw."

Those words have stayed with me all these years. How true it is! Jesus, in us, is the glorious One.

That's what II Corinthians 4:6-7 refers to:

For God, who commanded the light to shine out of darkness, hath shined in our hearts, to give the light of the knowledge of the glory of God in the face of Jesus Christ. But we have this treasure in earthen vessels, that the excellency of the power may be of God, and not of us.

I love milkshakes, so now I often tell people that praise me, "Oh thank you. Jesus is the milkshake, I'm the straw."

For years I attended Faith Community Church where Jess Slusher, the senior pastor, was wonderful about letting me share with the congregation what God was doing in my life. One time I got to share with them a little visual about this very thing.

I took several straws, a tiny coffee stirring straw, several regular straws, a flexible, bendable straw and a great big fat straw almost a half inch in diameter. The Lord had impressed upon me to demonstrate how those straws reflect our lives.

We can choose what size straw we want to be. If we only concentrate on our own concerns and the concerns of the world, we'll be about the size of the tiny one. If we spend a great deal of time allowing God to conform us to the image of Jesus, we'll be a much bigger straw that allows many more people *to taste and see that the Lord is good* (Psalms 34:8).

The Lord also instructed me to demonstrate how we can allow our straws to get all bent out of shape by anger, bitterness, and unforgiveness. I crumpled a straw in my hands so that the bent twisted straw was almost useless to deliver a drink.

God also had me stuff a straw, so that it was plugged; to show that we can also let things clog our lives. We mustn't let fear or pride or love of other things plug our straws, if we want others around us to really get to experience Jesus Christ in all His goodness and glory. The bendable straw was used to show that we can be flexible to reach even more people!

What a privilege to be indwelt by God's very own Spirit. What an honor to be used to help others experience the life giving water of God's Word (Ephesians 5:26).

He that believeth on [Jesus], *as the scripture hath said, out of his belly shall flow rivers of living water.*
John 7:38

The Double Arrow

*H*ere is a simple drawing that can have a huge impact on your life, if you take it to heart! On a blank page, perhaps in your Bible, write "BLESSINGS & FREEDOM" across the top of the paper. Across the bottom write "BONDAGE." Next draw an arrow from the top words to the bottom words and put a pointer on both ends of the arrow.

Now turn the paper so that the top edge is to your right. At the midpoint of the arrow, write the word "TRUTH" along the arrow pointing to the words blessings and freedom. Next, turn the paper 180 degrees, so that the top is to your left. At the midpoint of the arrow, write the word "LIES" so that it is along the arrow pointing to the word bondage.

This diagram applies to almost everything that you know about anything. Your understanding falls somewhere on that line. If you know the truth about something and are acting on that truth you'll be experiencing blessings and freedom in that area.

In any area where you are experiencing a lack of freedom, it's almost certain that somewhere along the way you have believed and acted upon a lie. That lie comes in many forms. Here are a few examples. "I'm worthless." "I never do anything right." "God won't help me." "Nobody cares about me." "It won't matter if I sin just this once." "I can't do anything about it." "Everyone in my family has this problem." "I can't change." "I can't do anything about it."

I challenge you to think of an area of your life in which you are *not* enjoying blessings and freedom. Prayerfully ask God to show you what lie(s) you've believed in that area. Now ask Him to show you the truth about the matter.

He will. That's what Jeremiah 33:6b reveals. The Lord declares, "[God] *will reveal unto them the abundance of peace and truth.*"

Start thinking and acting on the truth. You *will* move up the line from bondage to freedom.

For example, when I'm feeling anxious, I'll pray the way I've just described. Or when my husband and I are having a disagreement, I'll just stop and ask God to show me the lie that we have believed. Every time He comes through and His Word works!

You have just drawn a picture of what Jesus taught in John 8:32.

And ye shall know the truth, and the truth shall make you free.
John 8:32

The Double Arrow Drawing

BLESSINGS & FREEDOM

BONDAGE

I have not written unto you because ye know not the truth, but because ye know it, and that no lie is of the truth.
I John 2:21

License Plate Game

*M*ost experts agree that there are four primary personality types. I learned the big words in college, but when I was in my thirties, I heard them described as animals. That stuck! So here's a quick refresher course on personalities:

The Lion says, "Do it my way!"
The Beaver says, "Do it the right way."
The Otter says, "Let's do it the fun way."
The Golden Retriever says, "Let's do it your way."

I am an Otter and I love to make life fun as much as possible. God created me and He delights in giving this "otter" joy. One fun way that He showed me to praise Him is to play what I call the License Plate Game.

When I am travelling in a car, or walking through a parking lot, I look at the letters on a license plate. Then I use those letters to start words that describe and praise God. For example:

WUL becomes Wonderful Understanding Lord.
ZDJ becomes Zion's Deliverer Jesus.
MHG becomes Most Holy God.

Usually the words describing God pop into my mind really fast. But I still remember the time I was visiting my daughter, Rebekah, in Spokane during the time in her life that she was being very tempted to be drawn into the world's ways. I was fasting one day a week for her to overcome the temptation and be all that God created her to be. It was a huge concern to me.

During that time, at the end of one my visits with Rebekah, as I was heading for my car, I saw the letters GWR. Those three letters stumped me for a couple of moments and then God's Holy Spirit lovingly spoke to me, "God Watches Rebekah."

Praise God for being such a faithful, powerful, good Father who really does watch over His children with great care and tender love! I also praise God for understanding how much I like to play games.

I will praise thee, O LORD, with my whole heart; I will show forth all thy marvelous works.
Psalms 9:1

Don't Blame God!

My friend's daughter died of cancer after following different medical and alternative health procedures. She was a young mother who left behind a devastated husband and orphaned little ones. I grieve for the family. I'm not trying to add condemnation to anyone, especially in their time of grief. I *am* hoping to prevent others from experiencing unnecessary grief.

As I read my friend's words, "We all prayed for healing but God took her home, it must be God's will."

My spirit cried out, "Please don't blame God!"

Then God showed me a parable. Would anyone take a master chef's favorite recipe, substitute several ingredients, omit others, use their own time for baking, and then, when the dish was a disaster say, "Well, the chef must have wanted this?" Absolutely not! Yet that is exactly what people do to God!

Why do so many people just disregard the verses in the Bible about healing? They will even split a verse, believe part of it and totally disbelieve the rest of it, which is the part about healing. For example Psalms 103:2-3, *Bless the Lord, O my soul, and forget not all His benefits, who forgiveth all thine iniquities,* **who healeth all thy diseases.**

Thousands of people claim to believe God really does forgive *all* their sins and iniquities, but what about the rest of the verse "*who heals all your diseases?*" That is also part of the Divine Chef's master recipe. Healing has always been a very important thing to God.

In Exodus 15:26, we read that three days after God had parted the Red Sea for the Israelites, He told them how important healing was to Him and what the conditions were to get it:

> *If you will diligently hearken to the voice of the LORD thy God, and will do that which is right in His sight, and will give ear to His commandments, and keep all His statutes, I will put none of these diseases upon you which I have brought upon the Egyptians;* **for I am the LORD that heals you.**

During Jesus' time on earth, healing was a huge part of His ministry because it was so important to God. Again and again in the gospels, it is written that *Jesus went about...teaching...and preaching...and* **healing all manner of sickness and all manner of disease among the people.** Matthew 4:23 and Luke 9:11 are just two of many verses telling about Jesus' healing ministry.

There are two places in the New Testament that record why Christian Believers were stricken with disease and/or death by God. In Acts 5, the husband and wife lied about what they were giving to God and they were each killed instantly. Also, in I Corinthians 11:27-32, we are told that many people in the church were sickly or had died due to taking communion unworthily! We certainly need a healthy dose of awesome respect and fear for our holy God. [Savor Communion, pg. 175]

In I Corinthians 10, especially verses 6-10, we've also been given strong warnings about behaviors that resulted in many deaths of God's chosen people in the Old Testament. Then the next verse, I Corinthians 10:11, tell us that these deaths happened for examples and as warnings to us! I think that means we are to really listen and learn. Such destructive behaviors listed in those verses include: sexual sins, critically appraising God, and discontentedly complaining.

Do you know that there is not a *single* place in the Bible where Jesus told anyone that the sickness or disease was sent from His Father to teach somebody something, yet today that excuse is used by many. John 9:3 records that Jesus did say that the blind man was born blind, not due to sin, but so that the healing works of God should be shown in his life. Then Jesus healed the blind man who became a great witness for Him!

It is written in Matthew 13:58 that [Jesus] *did not many mighty works there because of their unbelief.* Unbelief was the culprit then and it still is now. Unbelief is one reason that we don't see God do mighty works.

Another cop out for not following God's powerful recipe for healing is when people bring up Paul's thorn in the flesh. My reply to that is, "Have you been caught up into the third heaven like Paul describes in II Corinthians 12:2-4?"

That is the reason Paul clearly tells us he was afflicted in II Cor. 12:7, *And lest I should be exalted above measure through the abundance of the revelations, there was given to me a thorn in the flesh, the messenger of Satan to buffet me. lest I should be exalted above measure.*

If you've been caught up into the third heaven and received revelations that are so magnificent that it's impossible to describe, (II Cor. 12:4), then you'd be qualified to have a thorn in the flesh like Paul did.

In Matthew 10:1 it is written that Jesus gave His disciples *power against unclean spirits, to cast them out, and to heal all manner of sickness and all manner of disease.* Before He ascended into heaven, Jesus' final instructions were to go into the world to preach, and teach them to observe *all* things that He had commanded, and to **heal**. (Matthew 28:19-20 and Mark 16:15-18).

Jesus also spoke powerfully to His followers just before He ascended into heaven saying, *All power is given unto me in heaven and in earth* (Matthew 28:18). The sad truth is that most people don't really believe Him and that's why we are not seeing His will being done.

God's recipe has not changed. Healing is still very important to God. He needs people to read and follow His complete recipe. We must stop believing the traditions of men, which explain away the miraculous power of God and replace it with a watered down explanation of why God can't, or won't, do anything today.

Yes He will! God's Word works! We must take responsibility to believe and obey His Word, and to resist the enemy. The early church clearly understood the good that God was wanting in their lives, and the evil that the devil wanted in their lives. They also did *not* blame God for what the devil was doing. The traditions of men have done great damage to people's faith in God and His power (Matthew 15:3).

The early Christians knew that, in this life on earth, we are all in a huge spiritual battle between the truth of God and the lies of the devil. The New Testament is filled with exhortations to be aware of the wiles of the devil, to resist the devil so he will flee from you, to fight the good fight of faith, and to use our shield of faith to quench all the fiery darts of the wicked. Those are still God's instruction to His people.

One wile of the devil is getting us to use our words for evil instead of good. Proverbs 18:21, in the Amplified warns us, *Death and life are in the power of the tongue, and they who indulge in it shall eat the fruit of it [for death or life]. [Matt. 12:37.]*

Be aware of your words, especially the slang sayings of the day, such as, "My back is killing me." "I could die for chocolate." "That makes me crazy." "That scared me to death." Those words are invitations for darkness and death to enter your life. Such words are definitely not part of God's divine recipe for health and godliness.

Henry Wright, in A More Excellent Way, explains that much disease is caused by a break down between man and God, man and others, or man and himself. There are consequences to our choices. We must take responsibility for our emotional and spiritual sins by confessing them and turning away from them. Henry Wright has helped countless people be healed from "incurable" diseases. He is a man who has learned some very powerful truths from God.

We'd be wise to pay attention to men and women who have learned about, and experienced, God's healing ways. We must seek to obey and follow God's way completely and believe that He is the Lord that heals us, before we will experience His divine recipe in all its health and glory!

Beloved, I wish above all things, that you may prosper and be in health, even as your soul prospers.
III John 1:2

He Needs Us

*O*ften just as I am waking up, the Lord speaks to my spirit and clearly impresses something upon me. This is an example of what's described in Psalms 143:8, *Cause me to hear thy loving kindness in the morning; for in thee do I trust. Cause me to know the way wherein I should walk; for I lift up my soul unto thee.*

I love those times of early morning revelation from my Lord. I remember a surprising message that came to me, one gloriously sunny morning while I was in Hawaii. I had just awakened and I was praising God. Then I felt in my spirit that God was saying "I need you to write the book."

I was excited and motivated to get busy and write more stories about what He had done in my life. Then moments later, doubt attacked. I began to wonder about what I had heard. Did God really *need* me to do anything? After all He's God!

So when in doubt I did what I've learned to do, I turned to the Bible. I asked God to please confirm what I thought that He had just told me, or if I was wrong to show me that. I prayerfully opened my Bible and the first verse that I saw was Matthew 21:3, *And if any man say aught to you, ye shall say, The Lord hath need of them; and straightway he will send them."*

Wow! I know that verse is actually referring to a donkey and her colt. But I am more than willing to be like Balaam's donkey who spoke what God told her to say (Numbers 22:27-34).

I think there are many of us that have been holding back on what we might be doing with God because we've believed some kind of a deceptive lie from the enemy. Those lies can come in several forms.

Here are a few of the most common discouraging lies we can hear: What do you have to offer? Who do you think you are? What about that time you really blew it? Why would God choose to use you? You're not (smart, strong, wise, young, old, etc. etc.) enough to do that.

Let's face it. In our own strength we really don't have much to offer a hurting broken world that desperately needs to see a living, loving, powerfully present God.

However, when we surrender to God, seek His will as revealed in His Word, and allow His Spirit to have His way, then it is no longer just us. As Philippians 1:21a says, *For me to live is Christ.*

That means that it is Christ [the One anointed with the Holy Spirit]] in us. That makes all the difference in the world!

I urge you to earnestly and expectantly seek what God wants to do in and through you. Then do it! Let's stop listening to the lies that defeat us.

Instead, let's listen to God. He wants us to say, *I can do all things through Christ which strengtheneth me* (Philippians 4:13).

I press toward the mark for the prize of the high calling of God in Christ Jesus.
Philippians 3:14

Sent to Help

I had just used up my package of Camas Prairie Tea and thought to myself, "I'll need to get some more, next time I go to Wenatchee." Then the Lord distinctly spoke, "Go to the health food store in Ephrata."

That surprised me, since the last time that I had been in there was several years ago and it was a rather oppressive place to me. However, God said, "Go." So, I went.

When I arrived I could see that the shelves were rather bare and there was only a young dark-haired man, who seemed very shy. Apparently he was running the place all by himself.

I saw that essential oils were on sale, so I used my cell phone to call my friend, Deb. She had just been introducing me to the various oils and I knew she could tell me which ones would be most useful to buy. She did. At the end of our call, I simply said, "God bless you, Deb."

As soon as I had hung up, the quiet young man approached me, and shyly said, "I didn't mean to be eavesdropping or anything, but I heard you say, 'God bless you.' Are you a Christian?"

"Oh yes." I answered. "Are you also a Believer?"

"Yes," he answered.

Then we began visiting. He explained that he and his mom had run the store since he'd been a little boy, but she had died about a year ago. He was broken-hearted, afraid, and entirely on his own. He was trying his best to keep it up, but he was about out of money and pretty overwhelmed.

The Lord gave me great compassion for that young man. I bought many things that day from his store so that he would have some money. I also prayed with him for guidance and God's perfect will in his life. Before I left the store, we exchanged phone numbers. He called me a few days later.

Over the next several months I got to watch God make huge changes in the young man's life. As it turned out, he didn't really like the store, but the lease was still in effect for a few more years, so he felt trapped. We prayed and God gave him favor with the landlord, who was willing to let him move out in one month, without penalty!

I suggested that he have a moving sale. He started with everything at 50% off. Each week it was increased to 60%, 70%, and so on. It lasted until the final week of his rent, when it was 90% off. I went to his store several days a week to buy things to help his cash flow. I also helped him clean the back of the store, where he had been living. Hiding was more like it.

The place was almost knee deep in junk and garbage. I suggested that he rent a huge dumpster and he did. We filled it several times and really got the place cleaned out! Of course, as we worked side by side, I told him what God had done in my life and what I'd been reading in my Bible that was pertinent to him. He began to understand how close and powerful God could be.

He had let fear so overwhelm him that he had just stayed there. He had been afraid to even go to the house his mom had owned for fear it would be repossessed.

I helped him learn about some local probate and tax laws. He was able to move into the abandoned home. He experienced peace. The young man's face had actually changed. His serious frown had relaxed. He had a light in his eyes, instead of dark fear and doubt.

I learned that he had never gotten his high school diploma. He was afraid that he couldn't pass the math sections. So, my husband and I helped him study math. He was very intelligent. I made the arrangements and he passed his GED with flying colors in a very short time.

With all his experience in retail, I suggested that he apply for a job at Wal-Mart. I encouraged him and we did mock interviews for practice. He got hired. Having a regular income without the worries and hassles of being an owner was a refreshing experience for him.

By then he had become like a son to us. He came over for dinners and to visit. We celebrated his birthday. He received a stocking and opened gifts with us on Christmas morning. He was overwhelmed with joy.

It was a delight to love a child of God the way I John 3:18, Amplified Bible describes, *Little children, let us not love [merely] in theory or in speech but in deed and in truth (in practice and in sincerity).*

What a wonderful transformation God had done in his life to set him free in so many ways. What a privilege to be sent to help.

The Spirit of the Lord God is upon me; because the LORD hath anointed me to preach good tidings unto the meek; He hath sent me to bind up the broken-hearted, to proclaim liberty to the captives, and the opening of the prison to them that are bound.
Isaiah 61:1

Encourager

$\mathscr{S}$ometimes God tells me to say something that will be hard for the listener to hear, I try to say it as honestly and gently as possible. Some people become very angry at me and I don't enjoy that, but it is more important to me to please God than it is to please people (Proverbs 29:25).

It's a wonderful joy when He gives me an encouraging message for someone. That was the case when we attended a B. J. Thomas concert in Spokane, Washington many years ago.

I have loved B. J. Thomas' upbeat music since I was a teenager. It was thrilling news to me, when he became a Christian in the mid 1970's! Then my heart went out to him, when I read one of his interviews a few years later.

In that article, he said that he could play a Christian song for a secular group and they would applaud; but when he sang a secular song at a Christian concert, he was booed. That brought tears to my eyes. What a shame that the very ones who claim to be the Body of Jesus could be so rude and judgmental. After reading that article, I prayed earnestly for B. J. Thomas to be healed from hurt, to be protected from cruel remarks, and to grow in his faith.

Years late, in Spokane, B. J. Thomas gave a magnificent performance. Afterwards, he graciously came down from the stage into the audience where many people went up to see him.

Then the Lord told me to go say a specific thing to B. J. Thomas. So, I went up and patiently waited as he very politely greeted and spoke with the people and signed autographs. When he approached me he seemed a little weary and looked at me questioningly, probably wondering if I also wanted an autograph.

I simply said, "I just want you to know that God says you're still the apple of His eye."

B. J. Thomas' face lit up, as he said, "Thank you. Bless you." Then he gave me a quick hug and a kiss on the cheek. I returned to my husband very glad that I had been obedient to cheer one of God's precious children!

And now, brethren, I commend you to God, and to the word of His grace,
which is able to build you up, and to give you an inheritance among all
them which are sanctified.
Acts 20:32

Healthy Grapes

*G*od showed me an important lesson while I was washing some grapes. The store had sold them in a plastic mesh bag. I opened the bag and dumped them all into a colander to clean them.

Then I noticed that all the grapes still attached to the stem were fine, but the loose ones were not in very good shape. I threw those away. That's when God showed me the similarities between grapes and people.

Jesus said, *"I am the vine, ye are the branches; He that abideth in me, and I in him, the same bringeth forth much fruit; for without me ye can do nothing,"* (John 15:5).

When we stay attached to Him and close to others who are attached to Him, it is much easier to stay spiritually healthy, vibrant, and alive. If we are separated from the vine, we will wither and die, it is just a matter of time.

That's what Jesus warned us in John 15:6, *If a man abide not in me, he is cast forth as a branch, and is withered; and men gather them, and cast them into the fire, and they are burned.*

It is not impossible to be a vibrant Christian when we are isolated from others, but it is much more difficult. Such a life demands incredible focus and a strong determination to stay very close to God rather than being pulled into the world's ways.

God wants all of His kids to be loved by His other kids. Togetherness makes it easier to be a healthy grape, or healthy Christian. Loving fellowship also makes life much more enjoyable.

This is my commandment, That ye love one another, as I have loved you.
John 15:12

Intimacy Anorexia

*A*lmost immediately after our wedding, I realized that something was very, very wrong, but I had no idea what it was and I figured that love could overcome anything. I also believed that God would enable us to do all things through Jesus Christ, and I knew God wanted us to be a loving husband and wife.

So, that's how we behaved in public. However, in private, when it was just the two of us, it was a much darker picture.

Having been raised by angry alcoholics, who were co-dependent on each other, I had baggage. I had also learned to be co-dependent. I was afraid of rejection and paralyzed by confrontation.

I was very insecure, except in my relationship with God. I knew beyond a shadow of a doubt that He really loved me and I adored Him!

I was very naïve when we got married. I figured everyone who said that they were a Christian was indeed a sincere, Bible believing and Bible obeying Christian. Unfortunately, I now realize how wrong I was.

I also had a huge desire to be the kind of wife that God wanted me to be. I'd only been a Christian for about two years when we were married. Having lived in the girls' dorm on campus during the school year and with my parents during the summers, I'd never even seen a godly married couple interacting.

I'd heard it said that most couples spend more time planning their wedding ceremony than they do their marriage. I didn't want that. So, I read everything I could find about godly marriages before we got married.

Unfortunately, one article I read gave some terrible advice. It said that a godly, submissive wife must never nag. That sounded right to me.

Then it went on to say that if a wife said anything more than once, it would be nagging. As preposterous as that may sound, that's the plan that I followed for the first seven years of our marriage!

I remember one day earnestly writing in my prayer journal to God that "something is really, really wrong in our marriage."

Combine a "Stepford wife" with an immature, self-centered guy, who wants to be treated as if he is perfect all the time, and you have quite a recipe for disaster. We certainly did.

The coldness, lack of love, and distance that Leigh kept was mind boggling. Coupled with the fact that in public, he'd act very attentive to me, it was very confusing and made it almost impossible to explain to anyone else, because they only saw the good behavior.

It was heartbreaking. However, since the first verse that God ever made "jump" off a page for me was Romans 8:28, *And we know that all things work together for good to them that love God, to them who are the called according to His purpose,* I always believed God could use the terrible situation somehow for good.

Looking back on almost 40 years, I do see that I have learned several important things. I have learned to dwell in the secret place of the Most High, where God shelters me from evil (Psalms 91). I've experienced countless times when my Lord really did heal my broken heart (Luke 4:18). I let the situation purify me. I learned to forgive over and over and not become bitter.

It seemed like every time I was at a breaking point, thinking that I couldn't take any more emotional abuse and cruelty, God would show me something that made a big difference in my life. One of those times was when He showed me a powerful truth from John 20:13-15.

That's where Mary is standing outside the empty tomb on Resurrection morning, but she has no idea where Jesus is. He's right there, but she thinks He's the gardener, even while He's talking to her. Then Jesus asked a penetrating question, in verse 15, *"Woman, why weepest thou? Whom seekest thou?"*

Jesus' questions caused me to realize that if I seek anyone else besides Jesus Christ and God the Father, sooner or later there will be times when I will feel like weeping. However, if I am truly seeking Him, there is no need to weep, except tears of joy!

Our marriage situation has really forced me to seek Jesus and to keep my focus on Him. It was the only way to avoid becoming bitter, insane, or fat.

Then another huge breakthrough happened a few years ago. I had registered to take some Christian counseling courses. One of the tuition benefits was a subscription to their magazine. As I looked through it, an ad "jumped off the page."

It was an ad from Heart to Heart Counseling Center in Colorado Springs, Colorado. The ad concerned intimacy anorexia materials.

I had never heard the term before and really had no idea what intimacy anorexia was. However, when the Holy Spirit prompted me to order the materials, I did.

Dr. Weiss, the director and author, hit the destructive, secretive nail on the head! For years Dr. Weiss has dealt with what he calls intimacy anorexia, where one spouse is addicted to willfully withholding emotional, spiritual, and sexual intimacy from the other spouse.

Dr. Weiss understood exactly how the secretive addiction manifests itself. And even more importantly, he knew how to deal with the situation.

He very clearly explained that if the addict is willing to do the work to overcome the addiction and if the spouse is willing to be healed, the couple can end up with a great marriage. His materials give many concrete practices for the addict, and great information and advice for both the spouse and the addict.

It is so much easier dealing with a difficult situation when you understand the truth about what is happening. I am so thankful that the Holy Spirit prompted me to order the materials.

And ye shall know the truth, and the truth shall make you free.
John 8:32

He's Behind the Curtain

*S*ometimes you don't even understand how important something that you learn in life will be, when you are first learning it. Then later you realize what an incredible thing that truth was.

That's just what happened to me. When I was a brand new Christian, in the early 1970's, Joy Dawson came to Montana State University in conjunction with Youth with a Mission.

I loved hearing her talk with her New Zealand accent. I especially loved hearing her talk about God! She was, and still is, a woman who knows God Almighty much better than most people ever know Him. She called Him the Lover of her soul.

During one session she explained that sometimes God will teach us something and then He is like a parent who will test their child to see if the lesson really has been learned. The parent may hide behind the curtain and watch to see what the child will do. The Father sees the child the entire time, even though the child is unaware of His presence.

She told us not to get upset if we didn't feel God's presence, just to know that He was probably behind the curtain, watching. That made sense to me.

A few days later, I wasn't experiencing God's presence as strongly as I usually did. I remembered what Joy taught. So, I laughingly said out loud to God, "Are You watching me from behind the curtain?

It was as if He came swooping out and gave me a big hug. I can honestly say that I know that I am ALWAYS in His presence. Where could you possibly go that He would not be there?

That's what Psalms 139:7-12 is all about—God is everywhere! So I just accept that fact and I enjoy the One Who has become the Lover of my soul too!

Whither shall I go from thy Spirit? Or whither shall I flee from thy presence? If I ascend up into heaven, Thou art there; if I make my bed in hell, behold, Thou art there.
Psalms 139:7-8

Guidance Prayer

Joy Dawson also taught about a wonderful way to get God's guidance on a matter. She explained that when we have an idea, it could be from our own mind, from our emotions, from the enemy of our souls, or from God. It's important to silence the first three, so that we can hear God's still small voice.

So, following her teaching this is how I have prayed for decades when it's time to get guidance on a matter in my life. First of all, to get guidance from God I must be utterly submitted to God. Since I really do want His way and I am willing to follow it, I tell Him just that and I usually use the two extremes of the issue.

For example if I am praying about giving something, I would tell God that I am willing to give it all, or nothing, or anything in between. If I was praying about going somewhere, I would tell Him that I am willing to go right now, or not at all, or whenever else He might want me to go.

Then I continue praying, "I lay down my human logic and my human emotions and desires, in Jesus' name."

I picture myself kneeling before God's throne and literally laying those things before Him. I see myself totally yielded to His perfect will, and willing to obey whatever He tells me.

Usually at this point of my prayer I feel real peace because often my logic and my emotions are at odds with each other. Therefore just stilling those and knowing that God's will is going to be done, gives me a great peace.

Next, because it is written in James 4:7, *Submit yourselves therefore to God. Resist the devil, and he will flee from you.* I pray, "I resist the enemy in Jesus' holy name and you shall flee."

Then I am just quiet and I wait to hear God's still small voice communicating to me. Waiting on the Lord is a very important step.

As an interesting side note, I recently asked my grown daughter, Rebekah, when she really began to feel like her Christian faith was her own and not just a reflection of mine. She said, "It was when we were homeschooling and almost every day you would have us take ½ an hour to just be still and listen to God. That's when He became so real to me."

Let's never forget that because God Almighty is real and alive, He does communicate to us. He knows just what it takes for each of us to hear Him.

After I hear that still small voice, or holy hunch, I will often go to my Bible and ask for confirmation. That's where I simply ask God to please confirm what I believe that He has told me and I open up my Bible and begin reading until He quickens something to me. Often it is the first verse that my eyes see!

Remember God is very willing and able to give us guidance. He wants and expects us to know His voice. Much of John chapter 10 is devoted to teaching us about knowing and hearing the Good Shepherd's voice.

And when [Jesus] *putteth forth His own sheep, He goeth before them, and the sheep follow Him: for they know His voice,* is how John 10:4 clearly explains it.

Let us therefore come boldly unto the throne of grace, that we may obtain mercy, and find grace to help in time of need.
Hebrews 4:16

Strength to Strength

*W*hen I was 35, my dad, a 53-year-old attorney, wanted to marry a 30-year-old client. Leigh and I sent Mom, who was a part time travel agent, several thousand dollars so she could retain an attorney for the divorce. It turned out that our helping my mom infuriated my dad.

While I was in Montana for a short visit, my dad called me to come to his law office. Then he proceeded to shout and call me every filthy name he could think of. His secretary came and closed his door. He had verbally abused me like that all my life, but for the first time in my life, I spoke back to my dad.

After his cruel, false tirade against me, I steadily looked him in the eye and I calmly replied, "Dad, I am none of those things that you just called me. I am a godly, kind, loving, joyful Christian lady."

He was stunned speechless that I had dared to confront him with the truth. I stood up and walked to the door. There I turned towards him and earnestly said, "May God have mercy on your soul."

He furiously stammered, "May God have mercy on *your* soul."

I answered, "Oh, He does." Then I left his office.

Soon Dad called. He wanted to talk to me at my mom's, where I'd been staying. Mom didn't want him in her place. I figured I'd talk to Dad outside. Days before we'd asked for police surveillance, due to Dad's temper.

God prompted me to call the police to inform them that my angry dad was coming and I'd be on the sidewalk talking to him. After calling, I got down on my knees to pray for protection and guidance.

While I was praying, the doorbell rang. I peeked through the peephole. I was surprised and relieved to see a policeman. How had he gotten there so quickly? He asked if the fat man in the car outside was my dad. I said, "I think so."

"I'll escort you," said the officer.

As we walked to the car, my dad saw the policeman. Then my dad glared at me with such hatred as he drove off with his nostrils flaring, veins bulging in his forehead, and uttering curses at me.

That was the last time that I saw my father for over 20 years. My parents divorced. Dad married the young client with four kids. He had nothing to do with me or my children. It was actually rather peaceful not having him in our lives. He was so filled with hurt and anger. His behavior often hurt others.

When I turned 50, God told me to send a Message Bible and a letter to my Dad. I did. I'd forgiven him and I had no bitterness or fear of him anymore. I sent him cards for his birthday and Christmas for the next five years. I never heard anything from him.

I was shocked when, in the fall of 2009, my sister called to tell me that our dad had been involuntarily committed to a mental health nursing home months prior. She hadn't seen Dad for years. She didn't want to get involved, but she gave me the institution's phone number.

I called several times, but they wouldn't let me talk to my dad. It turned out his wife had given strict orders for Dad to *not* be allowed to talk to anyone but her. She was in the process of becoming his legal guardian and conservator, and would control his finances.

At the time, I was seeking God's perfect will for what He wanted me to do about my Dad's situation. As I read the words in Psalms 84:7, *They go from strength to strength, every one of them in Zion appeareth before God*, the Word of the Lord came to me.

He said, "I want your dad to come live with you and Leigh. I will take him from strength to strength."

Thus began a twelve-month journey of incredible things that only God could do! I needed to find an attorney to help me win in a contested guardianship case, or Dad's second wife would have complete control over him, and she did not want him to have any contact with me, my sister, or my brother.

I was earnestly hoping that Dad could reconcile with each of his three children. I also hoped that he would learn about the saving power of God's love and Jesus' sacrifice.

After calling over a dozen lawyers in Montana, I found Curtis Thompson. When I explained the situation, he said, "I will take the case. I have a soft spot in my heart for your Dad. He helped me when I was just getting started as an attorney. But I need to tell you that this will be expensive and I don't think we'll win."

"I believe in miracles," I joyfully answered. He took the case.

It will take another book to describe all the miracles that God brought about. I was finally able to talk to Dad on the phone. The second time I called him, Dad proudly explained that he'd told the caseworker after our first call, "My daughter is a strong Christian lady."

I was amazed! I hadn't said a thing about the Lord, or my faith, in that first call. After not seeing me for over 20 years, that was what my dad remembered about me. I started calling him daily.

Then I visited my dad at the mental health nursing home several times. I learned that he was heavily over drugged. Dad spent most days in bed. He could barely get to the bathroom in his room using his walker. He was usually wheeled to meals in a wheel chair. The medical staff and psychiatric staff were adamant—Dad could not leave.

He'd been diagnosed with Lewy Body Disease, with Parkinson's symptoms and dementia. I realized that I could give him the care that he needed in my home. His wife fought against me becoming his guardian and taking him to Washington.

I had about 20 points that showed how neglected Dad had been in the institution by his wife. For example, his false teeth were still at their home. She had visited him about once a month for a couple of hours, but she never brought his dentures. So, for months he'd had to eat without them.

Dad's wife was recovering from a stroke that she'd had in April. It seemed to be a pretty clear case in my favor. Then one phone call from my attorney changed the scenario. He'd had many talks with the pro bono attorney that the wife had representing her.

Mr. Thompson had learned that years ago, long before the dementia had begun, my dad had written some hateful words about me in his will to cut me out of his will and life. The wife planned to use that against me to assassinate my character in court. My attorney would not put me through that. He asked if I still wanted to proceed in helping to get my dad out.

At that moment God's Holy Spirit helped me to be like Jesus Christ. I answered, "Yes, I'll proceed with the case to get Dad out of there and take care of him in my home." Even though my dad had hated me so much over the years, I could feel God's love for him.

Curtis Thompson was a wonderful, compassionate negotiator. He explained to the other attorney that I was definitely not after the rather small amount of money that my dad had. I truly just wanted to help my dad live out his life as healthily and joyfully as possible.

After hiring an independent psychiatrist to write a report for the court about my dad's condition, we had a very strong case for Dad to be released into my care. Leigh and I were on a cruise in November when I received the email that the court would approve Dad coming to live with us on the following Monday. We were overjoyed!

However, the Sunday morning before our court date, as our ship was docking; the wife went to the institution and demanded Dad's release! She took him to their home, where she had already said that both she and my Dad were in danger of being hurt by having him there!

Once again, God did several amazing things. I drove to their home and met Dad's wife. Dad had told her all the good things that I had done for him. She was very cordial towards me and we worked out a plan.

I would stay in their home for a week helping Dad. Next I would take Dad to Washington, to live with us for a month. Then I would return him to Montana for Christmas. I also invited Dad's wife to come visit us at Thanksgiving to see where Dad would be and how well suited our home would be for a place to stay while God strengthened him.

That was what we did. During the month that Dad lived with us, there was a wonderful transformation. We discontinued several powerful narcotic drugs. I fed my Dad very nutritious food. I walked with him several times every day and we swam in our heated indoor pool. Soon we were able eliminate the diabetes medications. He went from taking 22 daily medications down to six!

Even though I love to stay at home, almost every day I took him to town where he loved to drive the electric cart while we shopped. I was able to facilitate reconciliation between my Dad and my sister. I encouraged Dad to call his wife, friends, and family daily.

I had Dad help me prepare meals and bake healthy cookies. We visited continually. I played cards with him for hours every day. Leigh would play cards with us in the evenings. I read the Message Bible out loud to Dad before he fell asleep for naps or at night.

I did get up with him during the night. Dad needed help with using the toilet. For the first weeks, it was over two dozen times every night. Then we found a prescription that would calm his bladder so he could sleep better and we only got up about ten times every night.

When I was too exhausted, Leigh would take nighttime duty. We earnestly prayed for Dad's healing and Dad would agree with a hearty "Amen."

God kept His Word to me. When I took Dad back to Montana a month later, we went to his cardiologist. Using only a cane, Dad walked into her office about 100 pounds lighter than she had seen him a year ago. His cardiologist thought we had turned the clock back about fifteen years in Dad's life. That's what his wife said too and she was interested in growing closer to God.

So for the next eight months, I cared for my dad in my home or drove him 490 miles to Montana, where he'd stay for a week or two. Then I'd go get him and bring him back to our home. It was truly amazing to see how God took my dad from strength to strength. It was also a wonderful thing to see his wife reading her Bible and discovering how great God is!

For with God nothing shall be impossible.
Luke 1:37

No More Ativan

After getting my dad released from the mental health nursing care institution where he had been involuntarily committed for over four months, I was staying at his home helping him to get stronger and healthier, before bringing him to my home in Washington. Dad had been over drugged and was on 22 strong medications! Ativan was one of the first drugs that the Lord made me to know should be eliminated.

It's usually prescribed for anti-anxiety, but it can have serious side effects including difficulty breathing and confusion. Dad had sleep apnea, and was dealing with Parkinsonian symptoms including confusion. The negative side effects outweighed any positives in this case.

Dad had been receiving it at bedtime and thought it helped him sleep. However, I would get up with him during the night, because he was weak and scared and needed help. We were getting up over twenty times each night. So, I knew it was not helping him sleep!

The next night I did not give him any Ativan, when he went to sleep at about 9:30 p.m. Just as I was about to go to bed at 11 p.m., Dad woke up. After helping him to the toilet and back to bed, I suggested that we play cards until he was sleepy enough to sleep. Dad wanted an Ativan, but agreed to play cards when he realized that I was *not* going to give him any more Ativan.

I explained, "If it was really helping you, I would give it to you, but it isn't, so, we aren't going to use it anymore. I believe you'll be much healthier without it."

He taught me all kinds of different ways to play poker that night. We played with his poker chips just for fun, no money. After a couple of hours, I was getting very sleepy.

Finally, Dad said, "I think I can sleep now."

"Great;" I said and helped him get all tucked into bed. Like every bedtime, I read to Dad from the Message Bible until he fell asleep.

I went down the long hall to my bedroom. I could hardly wait to go to bed. I was almost asleep, when the Lord said, "Get up. Go stand at his bathroom door by the kitchen. Your dad's going to the kitchen to get the Ativan for himself. You need to intercept him and stop him."

I went and stood outside that door to his bathroom. It's a small bathroom with one door into his bedroom and another door into the hall right by the kitchen. I was very quiet.

Dad slowly opened the door. His shocked look at seeing me changed to a "caught with my hand in the cookie jar" look.

He asked, "What are you doing? How did you know?"

"I'm helping you kick Ativan," I replied, "The Lord told me to stand here. Now, let's play some more poker, until you're really ready to sleep."

Dad laughed, turned around, and shuffled back to his bed. We played until the wee hours of the morning, but he never did need or take another Ativan in all the months that I cared for him. Praise the Lord!

And thine ears shall hear a word behind thee, saying, This is the way, walk ye in it,
Isaiah 30:21a

Garden Gloves

My daughter, Rebekah, had given me a pair of beautiful, brown, leather gloves that went almost to my elbows. I loved wearing them when I worked on my rose bushes. They really protected my hands and arms from cuts and scratches.

One sunny spring afternoon I was wearing regular wrist-length leather gloves while working in the yard, when I heard the still small voice of God's Holy Spirit prompting me to "put on the long garden gloves that Rebekah gave you."

Since I wasn't working on my roses, I didn't plan to work in the roses that day, and I didn't want to walk back to the garage to get the gloves, I ignored the prompting. A moment later, I had several long scratches across my forearms from the branches that I was trimming.

That was just lazy, proud, human nature in me refusing to listen to God's holy prompting! Not only did I end up with scratches which would have been entirely avoided if I had obeyed right away, I also grieved God. I confessed, repented, and went to get the long gloves.

Just a quick side note, the original words that we translate into repent, actually involves three steps. First we must hate what we've done. Secondly, we must turn away from it. Thirdly, we must go a new direction. If we don't do all three steps, we haven't really repented, at least not in God's eyes.

Although my ignoring God's prompting may seem like a minor infraction to some, it was an example of II Kings 17:34a, which the Message Bible clearly states, *"They don't really worship God—they don't take seriously what he says regarding how to behave and what to believe."*

Isn't that something? God considers our obedience as real worship. Remember what Samuel the prophet, told Saul, the disobedient King of Israel, *"Behold, to obey is better than sacrifice, and to hearken than the fat of rams"* (1 Samuel 15:22b).

In other words, God thinks that our obedience is a very reliable indication of whether we're honoring Him. It carries more weight than any offering we might be giving at church, if we're acting disobediently!

Jesus made it perfectly clear that our obedience is connected to our love for Him in John 14:23, *Jesus answered and said unto him, If a man love me, he will keep my words: and my Father will love him, and we will come unto him, and make our abode with him.*

I really do want to worship God in every way possible. I do appreciate that He takes the time to tell me even little things that will make my life safer and happier. Once again I am amazed that we have such a personal, caring God, whose love and wisdom would prevent us from so much harm if we would only learn to listen and obey His Word!

Perhaps you'd care to join me in this short prayer:

Dear Lord, Please teach me to be quick to obey your promptings, in Jesus' name. Amen!

But this thing commanded I them, saying, Obey my voice, and I will be your God, and ye shall be my people; and walk in all the ways that I have commanded you, that it may be well unto you.
Jeremiah 7:23

God's Choices

I think I was expecting God to be mean and I am really ashamed of that. It began one day when I had a most delightful day doing simple things like cleaning my home, baking dessert bars for the neighbors, visiting with friends on the phone, and singing and dancing before the Lord with pure joy and thankfulness.

I hadn't spent very long in the Bible and I didn't write anything for this book. Then last night as I was falling asleep, praising God for such a delightful day, I felt impressed to tell God that I would ask Him first thing in the morning what He would like for me to do, rather than just spend another day doing what I enjoyed and enjoying His presence.

I know that God is love (I John 4: 8), and I believe that His plans for me are the best (Jeremiah 29:11), yet I must confess. As I was falling asleep, I had wonderment in the back of my mind concerning what thing God would choose for me to do.

I was actually bracing myself mentally and emotionally to do anything that He asked. Now I realize I was thinking it might be rather hard, which I think shows that I was believing a lie about God and His ways.

The very first thing I asked Him this morning was, "What would You like me to do today, dear God, in Jesus name?"

Instantly the answer came, "Love Leigh."

I was a little surprised that it was something so easy. We've been having a really wonderful time in our marriage with both of us being kind, unselfish, and thoughtful of each other. So, after cuddling, I got up and made him a great breakfast. Then I packed a good lunch for him, including a love note. I gave him hugs, praises, and words of respect before he left.

After Leigh had gone to work, I again asked God, "What is Your next choice for me to do?"

Immediately, the answer came, "Go for a walk with Janelle."

Janelle is a gentle, generous young lady that I met at a Bible study. She lives about two miles away and we usually try to meet in the middle to walk and talk for an hour or so twice a week.

I was delighted to get to be with her. It is one of those friendships that you know is of God because we both feel so blessed by each other every time we get to be together. Her children are school age, and she's is very receptive to the things I share that God has taught me.

I continued asking God what to do next all day long and He kept answering with great ideas. Later it was time to go outside and clean up the campfire area. We'd been trying to burn fruit tree branches for several days but they hadn't burned. I lit one match and it took off in a blaze and continued to consume everything in the fire pit. Thank you, Lord!

Then I was going to get the extra branches in the orchard to add to the fire and He distinctly told me, "No."

I took about two more steps, pushing the wheelbarrow towards the orchard and then realized that if I was only going to do what God chose today, going to the orchard would be disobedience. So, I parked the wheelbarrow, came inside, and worked on this book.

I read my emails for only 10 minutes and didn't get sucked into the time warp of at least an hour before I even know how long it's been. It was a really productive, refreshing, fun day. I know that I was pleasing my Heavenly Father and He was teaching me again just what a fantastic Father He is.

Then I realized that God is so much more wonderful and kind than we usually give Him credit for being. We've all fallen prey to the lie that God's way would be so difficult and hard, when actually, just the opposite is true. He really does delight in giving us tasks to do that give us pleasure and glorify Him.

That's what He's telling us in Jeremiah 29:11, *For I know the thoughts that I think toward you, saith the LORD, thoughts of peace, and not of evil, to give you an expected end.*

I can hardly wait to spend another day asking and responding to God's choices for me. I think this could be a very good way to spend every day.

Trust in the LORD with all thine heart; and lean not unto thine own understanding. In all thy ways acknowledge Him, and He shall direct thy paths.
Proverbs 3:5-6

Behold Jesus

*O*ne Sunday years ago, as I wondered what the sermon might be about. I remembered that the last several sermons had been telling the congregation what to do, without much effect or impact. Then I realized something important that I've tried to remember when I'm teaching Bible studies—lift up Jesus. Let people see Jesus as He is and they will *want* to do whatever it takes to get closer to Him.

If we lose sight of the One that our hearts should long for, all of our ways will be reduced to merely man's efforts at trying to be religious. What good does that do?

However, when we behold the Glorious One, and realize that certain activities can draw us to Him, and draw Him to us, then we embark on those activities with a passion. That determination will please the Father, who looks on our hearts. He will reward us with our heart's desire—being closer to Jesus and to the Father.

Perhaps this is also what Jesus meant when He said *"And I, if I be lifted up from the earth, will draw all men unto me,"* (John 12:32). Let's endeavor in every way we can to behold Jesus and to lift Him up, or exalt Him. He wants us to do that.

Do you remember Jesus' passionate prayer just before He went to the garden of Gethsemane where He was betrayed? It's recorded in John 17.

The entire prayer is remarkable, especially verse 24, *Father, I will that they also, whom thou hast given me, be with me where I am, that they may behold my glory, which thou hast given me; for thou loved me before the foundation of the world.*

He earnestly asked God to let us see Jesus in His glory, in the present tense, not some future time and place. That was really important to Jesus because He knew how wonderfully powerful it would be to us. I believe God answered this prayer of Jesus in the last book of the Bible, Revelation.

Look at the first verses in Revelation 1:1-2:

> *The Revelation of Jesus Christ, which God gave unto Him* [Jesus], *to show unto His servants* [us] *things which must shortly* [suddenly] *come to pass; and He* [Jesus] *sent and signified it by His angel unto His servant John, who bore witness of the word of God, and of the testimony of Jesus Christ, and of all things that he saw.*

Do you realize that Revelation has a unique promise in the 3rd verse of the first chapter? It states, *"Blessed is he that readeth, and they that hear the words of this prophesy, and keep those things which are written in it, for the time is at hand."* It is time to behold Jesus!

When John saw the glorified Jesus Christ, described in Revelation 1:11-16, do you know what John did? Revelation 1:17 tells us that he fell at Jesus' feet like a dead man!

Remember this is John, the beloved disciple, who was closer to Jesus than any other disciple. John was with Jesus during all the miraculous points of His earthly ministry. John was in the elite group that saw Jesus raise the dead daughter of Jairus, recorded in Mark 5:41 and Luke 8:54. John was one of three who got to see Jesus in His transfigured shining state on the mountain recorded in Matthew 17:2 and Mark 9:2.

As incredible as those moments were with Jesus, they were *nothing* like what John saw when he beheld Jesus Christ as He *is* today in such glory and majesty. One glimpse at Jesus and John dropped like a dead man, because of the glory and the power and the holiness. He couldn't get up until Jesus reached out to touch him and told him *fear not* (Revelation 1:17).

It's also very significant the way Jesus identified Himself to John in Revelation 1:8, *I am Alpha and Omega, the beginning and the ending, saith the Lord, who is, and who was, and who is to come, the Almighty.*

Jesus said that He *is*, was, and is to come. The first words are the ones that determine how we see Him. Too many people only see Jesus as the One who *was*, walking along the dusty roads in Israel 2000 years ago. That doesn't have a really huge impact on most modern daily lives.

Jesus wants us to behold Him as He *is* now, seated at the right hand of His Father, God Almighty, because if we get even a glimpse of His Majesty we will be changed.

His glory will affect everything we do. I encourage you to behold Jesus.

But we all, with open face beholding as in a glass [mirror] *the glory of the Lord, are changed into the same image from glory to glory, even as by the Spirit of the Lord.*
II Corinthians 3:18

Powerful Prayers

*E*phesians has long been one of my favorite books of the Bible. It teaches the magnificent truth about the true Church, the Body of Jesus Christ. There is a glorious revelation about who we are in Christ that beckons me to live to that holy standard every time I read it. Especially in the last chapter, 6, there is strong teaching about how to live in the victory that Jesus Christ has made possible for us, if we will dare to believe and receive and achieve it!

Early in my Christian walk, a godly saint challenged me to pray the two prayers in Ephesians for myself every day for a month. I was also instructed to insert my name in the prayer. I took the challenge and did pray those two prayers every day for a month. It had a powerful effect on me.

I have since prayed these prayers for my children and for my husband. I believe you will also develop a glorious awareness in your life if you pray these prayers straight from the scriptures. Fill your name in the blanks.

Ephesians 1:17-23:

> I pray *that the God of our Lord Jesus Christ, the Father of glory, may give unto ____ the spirit of wisdom and revelation in the knowledge of Him, the eyes of ____'s understanding being enlightened; that ____ may know what is the hope of His calling, and what the riches of the glory of His inheritance in the saints, and what is the exceeding greatness of His power toward ____ who believes, according to the working of His mighty power, which He wrought in Christ, when He raised Him from the dead, and set Him at His own right hand in the heavenly places, far above all principality, and power, and might, and dominion, and every name that is named, not only in this age, but also in that which is to come; and hath put all things under His feet, and gave Him to be the head over all things to the church, which is His body, the fullness of Him that filleth all in all.*

Ephesians 3:14-21:

> *For this cause I bow my knees unto the Father of our Lord Jesus Christ, of whom the whole family in heaven and earth is named, that He would grant ____, according to the riches of His glory, to be strengthened with might by*

His Spirit in the inner man; that Christ may dwell in ____'s heart by faith; that ____, being rooted and grounded in love, may be able to comprehend, with all saints, what is the breadth, and length, and depth, and height, and to know the love of Christ, which passeth knowledge, that ____ might be filled with all the fullness of God. Now unto Him who is able to do exceedingly abundantly above all that we ask or think, according to the power that worketh in ____, unto Him be glory in the church by Christ Jesus throughout all ages, world without end. Amen.

I challenge you to pray these prayers for yourself and/or your loved ones for 30 days. I believe you'll be blessed.

There is one body, and one Spirit, even as ye are called in one hope of your calling; one Lord, one faith, one baptism, one God and Father of all, who is above all, and through all, and in you all.
Ephesians 4:4-6

It Is His Home

*H*ave you ever heard people discussing who gets into heaven? Some people don't think that God should keep out anyone that they think is just fine.

One day I was pondering those ideas and wondering how to answer people with something that they could understand and see God's point of view. Then it came to me.

If you were to visit my home, I would ask you to please take off your shoes before entering the living room where the carpet is new. I also would not allow you to smoke in my home. Those two things are very important to me.

I bet you have things that are important to you too about who comes into your home, and how, and when. For example, you'd probably rather they use the door, not a window.

Many verses refer to heaven as the place where God lives, just as Jesus prayed in Matthew 6:9, "*Our Father which art in heaven, Hallowed be thy name.*" Also, Job 22:12, "*Is not God in the height of heaven?*" Solomon prays to God in I Kings 8:30c, "*and hear Thou in heaven thy dwelling place.*"

Well, if we let people choose who comes into their homes, shouldn't God also be able to say who comes into His home? One time Jesus told the people to give Caesar what was his and to give God what was His (Matthew 22:21). I think that includes the respect that we give other people about how to enter into their homes. God certainly deserves at least that same respect.

Do you know anyone who always has an open invitation to everyone to enter into his home at any time? I don't, except God. He has the most welcoming, generous invitation of anyone I know. Yet there is a huge stipulation that is very important to Him.

We must come through His Son, Jesus Christ. God's great invitation is recorded in John 3:16, "*For God so loved the world, that He gave His only begotten Son, that whosoever believeth in Him should not perish, but have everlasting life.*"

Jesus also told us in John 14:6, "*I am the way, the truth, and the life; no man cometh unto the Father but by Me.*"

Often the rich and famous have attendants checking at their doors to make sure only the invited guests are the ones going in. God also has His invitation list, and only those named are the ones allowed into His home, or heaven. God's invitation list is called the Lamb's book of life.

Revelation 20:11-15 makes it very clear how vitally important being in the book of life is:

> *"And I saw a great white throne, and Him that sat on it...And I saw the dead, small and great, stand before God; and the books were opened; and another book was opened, which is the book of life. And the dead were judged out of those things which were written in the books, according to their works. And the sea gave up the dead which were in it; and death and hell were delivered up and the dead which were in them; and they were judged every man according to their works. And death and hell were cast into the lake of fire. This is the second death. And whosever was not found written in the book of life was cast into the lake of fire."*

The lake of fire was created to be the devil's final place. Unfortunately that is also where people will end up, instead of with God, in His heavenly home, if they do not want to enter God's home the way He chooses.

Let's be good guests who respect the Host, and enter into Heaven the way the Host has invited us. And let's try to get as many as we can to also have their name on the guest list in the Lamb's book of life.

And I John saw the holy city, new Jerusalem, coming down from God out of heaven, prepared as a bride adorned for her husband. And I heard a great voice out of heaven saying, Behold, the tabernacle of God is with men, and He will dwell with them and they shall be His people, and God Himself shall be with them, and be their God.
Revelation 21:2-3

A Five-Step Deliverance Prayer

This is a simple yet *powerful* way to deal with the spiritual battles that we all face. It is important in the spiritual realm to pray out loud. Be sure to go through all five steps, and be as specific as you can. You can be victorious!

Step 1:
Confess that I have let an unclean spirit lord it over me. Admit it is a sin since only God should be my Lord. Accept God's forgiveness and cleansing according to I John 1:9 and thank Him.

Example: "Dear God, I confess that I have let the spirit of (fear of failure) lord it over me and it's a sin, since only You should be my Lord. Please forgive me and thank You that it is written, *If we confess our sins, He is faithful and just to forgive us our sins, and to cleanse us from all unrighteousness.* Thank You for forgiving me and for cleansing me, in Jesus' name."

Step 2:
I announce Jesus is Lord of my life, Jesus is Lord of my thoughts, Jesus is Lord is of my words, Jesus is Lord of my emotions, Jesus is Lord of my choices, and Jesus is Lord of my actions.

Step 3:
I renounce the unclean spirit of (fear of failure) in Jesus' holy name. It has no right to lord it over my blood bought life.

Step 4:
Resist the unclean spirit of (fear of failure) according to the authority given to me in the Scripture (James 4:7).

Example: "It is written, *Submit yourselves to God. Resist the devil, and he will flee from you.* So, according to the authority given to me in Scripture, I resist you spirit of (fear of failure) and all unclean spirits associated with you in Jesus' holy name, and you shall flee."

Take a deep breath and exhale completely. Sometimes there will be a cough, or yawn, groan, sneeze, etc. That's fine, let it out.

Step 5:
I ask God to fill me with His Holy Spirit of courage, hope, love, etc. Usually it will be the opposite of the unclean spirit that was just resisted. Praise God!

A word to the wise—your deliverance, forgiveness and cleansing can happen immediately. Now decide to remain free by becoming spiritually mature which takes time and diligence.

Spend time studying God's Word. Look up verses about your situation. Memorize key verses that will help you to be an overcomer. Choose to obey God's Word. Spend time learning the wiles of the enemy of your soul and learn how God *always* has a way for you to go from victory to victory, without succumbing to temptations (I Corinthians 10:13).

However, if you do succumb, then start over again. Pray the five-step deliverance prayer.

Ye are of God, little children, and have overcome them: because greater is
He that is in you, than he that is in the world.
I John 4:4

Game Changer Definition

*S*ometimes there seems to be contradictions in the Bible. Usually a clearer understanding of the original text will clear up the misunderstandings. That was the case for me in a huge game changing manner.

I could clearly understand what Galatians 3:26-28 states, *For ye are all the children of God by faith in Christ Jesus. For as many of you as have been baptized into Christ have put on Christ. There is neither Jew nor Greek, there is neither bond nor free, there is neither male nor female; for ye are all one in Christ Jesus.* That makes it quite clear that there is no superiority between genders as Believers in Christ Jesus, from God's point of view.

I also knew that women held positions of authority in the Old Testament, such as Deborah, who was a prophetess and judge in Judges, chapters 4-5. Then there was Huldah, a prophetess that gave Hilkiah, the priest, and members of the king's officers, important instructions from the Lord, (II Kings 22:14, II Chronicles 34: 22).

There were several women, mentioned by name in the New Testament, who were spiritual leaders. Some examples include Phebe, Priscilla, and Junia.

Paul was inspired by God's Holy Spirit to write in Romans 16:1-2, *I commend unto you Phebe our sister, which is a servant* [diakonos, which is translated deacon in other places in the Bible] *of the church which is at Cenchrea: that ye receive her in the Lord, as becometh saints, and that ye assist her in whatsoever business she hath need of you; for she hath been a succourer of many, and of myself also.* So, Phebe was a deaconess who greatly helped Paul and many others.

Junia, a female name, is mentioned in Romans 16:7, as an apostle or noted among the apostles. *Salute Andronicus and Junia, my kinsman, and my fellow prisoners, who are of note among the apostles, who also were in Christ before me.*

It was obvious that women were praying and prophesying in the New Testament Church gatherings. I Corinthians 11:5, instructs, *But every woman that prayeth or prophesieth with her head uncovered dishonoureth her head; for that is even all one as if she were shaven.*

Then later in I Corinthians 11:15, it is written *But if a woman have long hair, it is a glory to her; for her hair is given to her for a covering.* That's the reason that I have always let my hair be long. I truly desired to please God and be obedient in all things.

So, I was confused when I read I Timothy 2:11-13, *Let the woman learn in silence with all subjection. But I suffer not a woman to teach, nor to usurp authority over the man, but to be in silence. For Adam was first formed, then Eve.*

Did that mean that a woman couldn't speak in church? That contradicted the earlier scriptures. Also, I wondered, "What on earth does Adam being created first have to do with a woman teaching?"

I knew there had been several times that God's Holy Spirit had prompted me to share something with a church congregation and I had. Men and women had been touched and encouraged, and thanked me for speaking.

Yet, I was in so much confusion about I Timothy 2:11-12, that I felt awkward when the husbands started attending a Bible study that I was leading among their wives. I wasn't sure I should be teaching men.

Then God cleared it up for me. My friend, Mary Catherine, gave me an article that explained the original text definitions. I checked in my Strong's Complete Dictionary of Bible Words and my copy of Expository Dictionary of New Testament Words to verify the information.

As it turns out, when Paul was inspired by God's Holy Spirit to write, *Let the woman learn in silence with all subjection* (I Tim. 2:11), he was actually giving women a wonderful invitation to learn. They were in cultures where women had not been allowed to be educated.

He was inviting them to learn just as men were to be learning in those days, with respectful, peaceful submission to the teacher. The word translated "in silence" in the KJV is the original Greek word, *hesuchia*, which is translated as "undisturbed or peacefulness" in other places in the Bible. So a woman could also learn in undisturbed peacefulness, not being afraid of what others thought about her.

If Paul had meant to put the women to silence, like to muzzle them, or stop all talking, he would have used a form of the Greek word *phimoo*. That implies forcing someone to be quiet like in I Peter 2:15, where we are instructed, *For so is the will of God, that with well doing ye may put to silence the ignorance of foolish men.*

There's more good news when we examine the original text! Paul was inspired to write to Timothy to give sound doctrine and to correct over 20 false teachings that were going on at that time, especially in Ephesus, where Timothy was. That's where goddess worship and Gnosticism were very prevalent. Goddess worship involved giving women credit for creating men.

With that in mind, let's look at the definitions of the words translated in I Tim. 2:12, *to teach nor to usurp authority over.* "To teach" comes from the Greek *didasko*. The conjunction "nor" is from the original Greek *oude* which shows a similarity rather than a distinction between two things.

The real game changer is the Greek word *authentein*. That word has four definitions in Greek: 1) to create or author, 2) to usurp, 3) to rule or dominate, and 4) to claim authorship or origination. Translators chose the second definition, "to usurp." But what if Paul was intending the first definition? The fourth definition is also quite similar to the first one.

That would make his instructions to people in a place where women were falsely being elevated to goddesses and taking credit for creating men, very meaningful. Those two definitions would give I Tim. 2:12 this type of translation, "I do not permit a woman to teach or to claim that she is the author or creator of men."

Not only does that make wonderful sense in disputing the prevailing errors, it also explains why the next verse, I Timothy 2:13 declares, *For Adam was first formed, and then Eve.* He was clearly showing that Adam was not created by any woman!

Also using those definitions of *authentein,* does not make Priscilla a violator of God's Word when she and her husband, Aquila, instructed Apollos in the deeper, and more complete things of God in Acts 18:26. As a result of what Aquila *and* Priscilla taught Apollos, he became a mighty force in the Body of Christ in the first century!

Paul also commended Timothy's mother, Eunice, and his grandmother, Lois, for having the unfeigned faith in God (II Timothy 1:5). Paul implied that it was a good thing that they had instructed Timothy about that faith.

I am excited that the Body of Christ is awakening to the truth in this matter. A wonderful pastor of a huge church in Asia once declared that the Church in America would never be as strong as God wanted it to be, until women were allowed to take their rightful place in the Body.

Some ministers are beginning to teach the truth which allows a woman to be obedient to God's Holy Spirit and to teach and exhort His Body. I believe there will be some glorious breakthroughs when this truth permeates the true Church.

And the servant of the Lord must not strive; but be gentle unto all men,
apt to teach, patient, in meekness, instructing those that oppose
themselves; if God peradventure will give them repentance to the
acknowledging of the truth;
II Timothy 2:24-25

Savor Communion

*W*ebster's Dictionary defines communion as spiritual intercourse; act of communing together spiritually or confidentially. Is that how you view communion? Or do you think of Communion as a cracker and juice?

Here's how I celebrate this intimate time with my Creator and Redeemer. I do this almost daily in my own home, usually alone, but sometimes with family or friends. First, I get the "bread" and the "cup."

Then I take time to see if there's anything in me that's grieving God, such as any wrong thoughts or harsh words. I ask Him to show me. This is so important. I Corinthians 11:28-32, explains that *many* of the Corinthian Believers were weak, sick, and even had died because they had not taken communion correctly by examining themselves and judging their own sin as sin. Do you think it's any different in our day and age? I don't.

Next I thank God, *that when I confess my sins, He is faithful and just to forgive me my sins and to cleanse me from all unrighteousness* (I John 1:9). I let that wash over my soul.

Then I take the "bread" and read I Corinthians 11:23-24, *"... the Lord Jesus, the same night in which He was betrayed, took the bread; and when He had given thanks, He broke it, and said, Take, eat; this is My body, which is broken for you: this do in remembrance of Me.* [Can't you see the loving tender heart of Jesus? He was ready to be beaten and to die for us, and He asked us to remember Him. That seems like the least we can do.]

I remember Him by reading Isaiah 53:4-5, *"Surely He hath borne my griefs, and carried my sorrows.. He was wounded for my transgressions, He was bruised for my iniquities; the chastisement for my peace was upon Him, and with His stripes I am healed."*

Then I eat the bread and think about all He has provided for me, joy instead of grief, mental peace instead of confusion, and physical healing because Jesus was beaten. I consider what a *huge* price He has paid!

The final step is when I take the "cup" and read Jesus' words in Matthew 26:28, *For this is my blood of the new testament, which is shed for many for the remission of sins.* As I drink from the cup I tell myself, "Jesus' blood makes it just as if I'd never sinned!" Wow!

Even if I do this daily, it never gets old. Communion is great for experiencing how much Jesus has done to give me abundant life, right now, and for all eternity.

For as often as ye eat this bread, and drink this cup, ye do proclaim the Lord's death till He come.
1 Corinthians 11:26

Anticipation

I just booked tickets for two upcoming trips and I am so excited and filled with anticipation. Then the Lord showed me several things.

My first trip is to Hawaii. My anticipation for Hawaii mirrors my anticipation of going to Heaven. I love how gorgeous Hawaii is with balmy blue skies, white puffy clouds, breaking turquoise waves on the sandy beaches, and the profusion of colorful tropical flowers.

I feel so close to God every time I'm in Hawaii. To me, the waves washing up on the beach sound like God breathing. His handiwork is seen, smelled, and tasted everywhere. I wouldn't be surprised if the Garden of Eden was very much like Hawaii, except for the rain showers. (I believe they didn't start until the flood in Noah's lifetime.)

To me there is such a peace in Hawaii. "Aloha" means the breath of life be with you. The breath of life is God Almighty's Holy Spirit. How could you *not* have Him present when you have thousands of people daily calling out "the Breath of Life be with you?" The power of life is in our words (Prov. 18:21). Even if most of the people saying "Aloha" have no idea of the real meaning of the word, God certainly does! And He responds.

My anticipation for my second trip also mirrors heavenly anticipation for a different reason. I'm going to Detroit, to spend a week with my dear friend, Cindy, who loves me. She truly sees the best in me. She showers loving kindness upon me. We communicate heart to heart. I believe that's what heaven will be like—a place where we are wonderfully loved and understood.

There is another similarity between booking my trips and going to heaven. My trips were booked with free points from airlines. They are gifts to me!

Going to heaven is also a gift to us from God, we *can't* earn heaven. We must simply accept the generous offer that God has made to us through Jesus Christ, His Son, paying for our eternal salvation with His death at Calvary.

I John 5:11-12 tells us, *And this is the record, that God hath given to us eternal life, and this life is in His Son. He that hath the Son hath life, and he that hath not the Son of God hath not life.*

There is one more important similarity. The free points were in my account, but I wasn't going to be taking any trips with those points until I believed that those points were good for a free trip and I appropriated them to get my free trips, according to the airline's stipulations.

God also has some stipulations. The sacrifice of Jesus is enough for every single person, but only those who really believe and receive Jesus' free gift will be going to heaven. Note what Jesus said in Matthew 26:28, *For this is my blood of the new testament, which is shed for many for the remission of sins.*

I have under lined Jesus' words to emphasize that it is *not* for everyone, but for many, who come to God through the narrow gate of faith in Christ Jesus, not the wide path the world offers (Matthew 7:14).

For those who go God's way, receiving the gift offered by Jesus' death and resurrection, there will definitely be a trip to a breathtakingly beautiful place filled with love. Oh, the anticipation!

And after these things I heard a great voice of many people in heaven, saying, Hallelujah! Salvation, and glory, and honor, and power, unto the Lord, our God.
Revelation 19:1

Made in the USA
Columbia, SC
25 July 2021

42216573R10098